exam success

(in)

ACCOUNTING

for Cambridge IGCSE® & O Level

Oxford excellence for Cambridge IGCSE® & O Level

OXFORD
UNIVERSITY PRESS

OXFORD
UNIVERSITY PRESS

Great Clarendon Street, Oxford, OX2 6DP, United Kingdom

Oxford University Press is a department of the University of Oxford. It furthers the University's objective of excellence in research, scholarship, and education by publishing worldwide. Oxford is a registered trade mark of Oxford University Press in the UK and in certain other countries

British Library Cataloguing in Publication Data
Data available

978-0-19-844475-6

5 7 9 10 8 6

Paper used in the production of this book is a natural, recyclable product made from wood grown in sustainable forests. The manufacturing process conforms to the environmental regulations of the country of origin.

Printed and bound by CPI Group (UK) Ltd, Croydon, CR0 4YY

Acknowledgements

The publisher and author would like to thank the following for permission to use photographs and other copyright material:

Cover: ESB Professional/Shutterstock

Illustration by Flash Harold Ltd

IGCSE® is the registered trademark of Cambridge Assessment International Education. All examination-style questions and answers within this publication have been written by the authors. In examination, the way marks are awarded may be different.

This Exam Success Guide refers to the Cambridge IGCSE® Accounting (0452) and Cambridge O Level Accounting (7707) Syllabuses published by Cambridge Assessment International Education.

This work has been developed independently from and is not endorsed by or otherwise connected with Cambridge Assessment International Education.

Contents

Unit 1: Introduction to accounting		**13**
1.1	**The fundamentals of accounting**	14
1.1.1	Bookkeeping and accounting	14
1.1.2	The accounting equation	16
	Raise your grade	18
Unit 2: Sources and recording of data		**22**
2.1	**The double-entry system of bookkeeping**	23
2.1.1	The double entry system of bookkeeping – an outline	23
2.1.2	Balancing and closing accounts	28
2.2	**Business documents and books of prime entry**	31
2.2.1	Business documents	31
2.2.2	Books of prime entry	32
	Raise your grade	37
Unit 3: Verification of accounting records		**45**
3.1	**The trial balance**	46
3.1.1	Uses and limitations of a trial balance; preparing a trial balance	46
3.1.2	Errors not revealed by a trial balance	48
3.2	**Correction of errors**	49
3.2.1	Types of error and their correction	49
3.2.2	The suspense account	50
3.2.3	Correcting financial statements	51
3.3	**Bank reconciliation**	54
3.3.1	Bank statements	54
3.3.2	Updating cash books	54
3.3.3	Bank reconciliation statements	56
3.4	**Control accounts**	57
3.4.1	The role and use of control accounts	57
3.4.2	Control account formats	60
	Raise your grade	62
Unit 4: Accounting procedures		**76**
4.1	**Capital and revenue**	77
4.1.1	Capital expenditure and revenue expenditure	77
4.1.2	Capital expenditure and revenue receipts	78
4.1.3	The effect of incorrect treatment of revenue and capital items on profit and asset valuations	79
4.2	**Depreciation**	80
4.2.1	Depreciation: background	80
4.2.2	Ledger and journal entries to record depreciation	82
4.2.3	The disposal of a non-current asset	85

4.3	**Adjustments**	87
4.3.1	Expense adjustments	87
4.3.2	Income adjustments	92
4.4	**Irrecoverable debts and provision for doubtful debts**	95
4.4.1	Irrecoverable debts and recovery of debts written off	95
4.4.2	Recording irrecoverable debts	96
4.4.3	Recording recovery of debts written off	97
4.4.4	Provision for doubtful debts	97
4.4.5	Recording provision for doubtful debts	98
4.5	**Valuation of inventory**	100
4.5.1	The rule for the valuation of inventory	100
4.5.2	The effects of an incorrect valuation of inventory	102
	Raise your grade	103
Unit 5: Preparation of financial statements		**119**
5.1	**Sole traders**	120
5.1.1	Sole trader background	120
5.1.2	Statements of financial position	123
5.1.3	Adjustments and the income statement	125
5.2	**Partnerships**	126
5.2.1	Advantages and disadvantages of forming a partnership	126
5.2.2	Partnership agreements	127
5.2.3	Financial statements	128
5.2.4	Format for partners' ledger accounts and financial statements	129
5.3	**Limited companies**	132
5.3.1	The background to limited companies	132
5.3.2	The financial statements of a limited company	134
5.4	**Clubs and societies**	137
5.4.1	Receipts and payments accounts and income and expenditure accounts	137
5.4.2	Revenue-generating activities	138
5.4.3	Income and expenditure account format	141
5.5	**Manufacturing accounts**	143
5.5.1	Direct and indirect costs, factory overheads and prime cost	143
5.5.2	Work in progress; calculating cost of production	144
5.5.3	Preparing the annual financial statements of a manufacturing organization	145
5.5.4	Adjustments to financial statements	148
5.6	**Incomplete records**	150
5.6.1	Disadvantages of not keeping a full set of accounting records	150
5.6.2	Preparing income statements and statements of financial position from incomplete information	152
5.6.3	Using ratios to find missing information	154
	Raise your grade	156

Unit 6: Analysis and interpretation	**187**
6.1 **Calculating ratios**	188
6.1.1 Importance of ratios and profitability ratios	188
6.1.2 Liquidity ratios	189
6.2 **Interpretation of accounting ratios**	190
6.2.1 Comparing results for different years	190
6.2.2 Users of accounting information; limitations of inter-firm comparisons and financial statements	193
Raise your grade	196

Unit 7: Accounting principles, policies and standards	**203**
7.1 **Accounting principles, policies and standards**	204
Raise your grade	208

| **Glossary** | 211 |

 Please go to **www.oxfordsecondary.com/esg-for-caie-igcse** for the answers to the 'Apply' questions.

How to use this book

Matched to the latest Cambridge assessment criteria, this in-depth Exam Success Guide brings clarity and focus to exam preparation with detailed and practical guidance on raising attainment in IGCSE® and O Level Accounting.

This Exam Success Guide:

- is fully matched to the latest Cambridge IGCSE® and O Level syllabuses

- includes comprehensive **Recap** and **Review** features with a focus on key course content

- equips you to **Raise your grade** with sample responses along with advice on the approach to take and key points to consider.

- includes **Common error** sections with information on how to avoid the mistakes students commonly make

- will help you to understand exam expectations with **Exam tips**

- equips you to test your knowledge with **Apply** questions and answers available online

- provides **Revision checklists** which enable you to build a record of your revision

- is perfect for use alongside the *Essential Accounting for Cambridge IGCSE® & O Level Student Book* (third edition), or as a standalone resource for independent revision.

This Exam Success Guide has been carefully designed to maximize exam potential. The features which will help you include:

- **You will need to know how to:** this is a list which appears at the start of every section and summarizes the key things you need to know for each topic.

- **Key terms:** definitions of the key terms and concepts are given the first time the term is used in the book. Many of these terms also appear in the **Glossary**.

- **Recap:** this section of the book recaps the key content with easy-to-digest points.

- **Exam tips:** these give clear details on how to maximize marks in the exam.

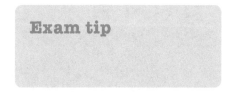

- **Common errors:** these notes give an indication of areas of the syllabus where students commonly struggle. By looking closely at these, you should avoid making similar mistakes in your exam.

- **Apply:** these sections provide targeted exam-style questions for you to answer. They have been written specifically for this Exam Success Guide and will help you to apply your knowledge and understanding in the exam. Answers to these questions are available online.

 Please go to **www.oxfordsecondary.com/esg-for-caie-igcse** for the answers to the 'Apply' questions.

- **Review:** at the end of each section of the book, you can review and reflect on the work you have done and find advice and guidance on how to further refresh and deepen your knowledge and understanding. This includes references to the Student Book.

- **Raise your grade:** a section appears at the end of each of the seven units. This section includes exam-style questions, with advice on what approach to take, then notes on how to check your answer. Sample multiple-choice questions and structured questions are included, so that you can practise each type of question.

- **Revision checklist:** a checklist appears at the start of each unit and can be used to record your revision.

How will you be assessed?

All candidates take two papers for the IGCSE® and O Level Accounting exam: Paper 1 and Paper 2.

Paper 1, multiple choice questions (1 hour 15 minutes)

There are 35 multiple choice questions, each worth 1 mark, making a total of 35 marks. This paper represents 30 per cent of the total marks.

Paper 2, structured written paper (2 hours 15 minutes)

There are five compulsory questions which carry 20 marks each, making a total of 100 marks. This paper represents 70 per cent of the total marks.

Assessment objectives

There are three assessment objectives (AOs). These are:

- knowledge and understanding (AO1)
- analysis (AO2)
- evaluation (AO3).

AO1: Knowledge and understanding

You should be able to:

- demonstrate knowledge of the facts, terms, principles, policies, procedures and techniques in the syllabus
- demonstrate understanding through numeracy, literacy, presentation and interpretation and apply this across a variety of accounting situations and problems.

AO2: Analysis

You should be able to:

- select data which is relevant to the identified needs of a business
- organize, analyse and present information in the appropriate format.

AO3: Evaluation

You should be able to:

- interpret and evaluate accounting information and draw reasoned conclusions.

Assessment structure

Assessment objective	%	%	%
AO1 Knowledge and understanding	80	60	65
AO2 Analysis	20	25	25
AO3 Evaluation	0	15	15

Aiming for success

Here are some ideas about how you can achieve the best possible mark in your Accounting exams.

During your course of study

Let's start with some ideas about how to make good use of your study time.

Research shows that there are some important things you can do from the very start to make sure you achieve your best. The first thing is to set yourself some definite goals.

Consider the following questions:

1. **What grade do you want to achieve?**
   Think about what you would need to achieve in order to feel pleased with your result and to ensure you can gain acceptance for the next stage in your education or employment. Setting a specific goal will motivate you and give you something to focus on.

2. **How much time do you spend outside of lessons working on developing your skills in Accounting?**
   Maybe you already spend a good many hours in private study, but if this is not the case, it is a good idea to make definite plans to increase your study time. This can be done gradually – for example, you could plan to add an extra hour to your normal study time for the next few weeks. Then you could add an extra hour to this, and so on.

Here are two more questions which may help you to think a little differently about how to approach your work:

3. **How do you feel when you have received some marks for your work in Accounting and you have not done quite as well as you hoped?**

   Many students will, understandably, answer by saying they are a bit deflated and hope they can get over the disappointment quickly. However, if this is your typical response, perhaps you could think a little differently. Students who look carefully at their mistakes and study the relevant material again can turn a negative experience into something more positive, which leads to real progress.

4. **What do you do with all your notes and other work from during your course of study?**

   Many students would find it helpful if they kept a more carefully organized collection of the work they do. Have a separate section for each topic with your notes, all the answers you have prepared together with the questions (or at least a reference to where the questions can be found). When it comes to preparing for the exam, having a well-organized file will mean you can get on with revision without wasting time trying to find the relevant materials.

Before you embark upon your revision, you should have:

- a definite goal – the grade you would like to achieve
- a plan to increase the time spent on private study
- a positive attitude and approach toward learning from any mistakes
- a well-organized file of work which will be invaluable for revision.

Effective learning and revision

Self-assessment

Self-assessment means that you mark your own work using a model answer or mark scheme provided by your teachers. There are many benefits to doing this if you carry out the process frequently, for example:

- You find out for yourself how well you have done as quickly as you wish after completing a task.

- You can get immediate information about any errors or omissions in your answer, so you can start to learn from your mistakes right away.

- If you use mark schemes, you can learn a lot about how marks are allocated to answers so that you are better prepared to produce the answers expected in an exam situation.

'Repairing' your answers

The more substantial benefits of checking your own work arise when you then go on to look more closely at any aspect of your answer which was not correct or where something was missing.

It is a good idea to spend a little time trying to understand why the model answer is showing an answer which is different from the one you have provided:

- Try to work out for yourself how the right answer was achieved.

- Ask your teacher or a friend to explain the right answer to you if you find it difficult to see how it was achieved.

- Try adding some notes about the correct answer; these notes will be useful when you look back at your work. This approach can be used for short questions requiring accounting techniques and for any prose answers.

There are reminders throughout this Exam Success Guide about repairing your answers.

Research has shown that the approach outlined above, when carried out systematically, can make a big difference to what students can gain from all the practical work carried out over a course of study. It can boost a student's performance by as much as two grades.

Revision

As the exams draw nearer, you will be thinking about the best way to revise. Just how much revision is done and how frequently it is done will, of course, vary from one student to another.

In Accounting it is important that a substantial portion of your revision time is spent answering questions. This will ensure you are skilled in carrying out the required techniques or you remember the key points to be made in a variety of questions requiring a prose response.

Effective learning and revision

Working through the topics

You may find it useful to make a checklist of all the main topics in the IGCSE® or O Level specification and work your way through the list, finding questions to try on each topic. This is where a well-organized course file will prove invaluable, because you should easily be able to find suitable questions with your answers, including your own notes on points you learned when you did the question originally, plus a model answer.

If you feel confident about a topic:

- Try the trickier parts of the related questions again.

- Avoid looking at the model answer unless you are finding it very difficult to find the answer yourself.

- Don't overlook answering some questions requiring a purely prose response, as well as those requiring accounts, calculations, financial statements, etc.

If you are less sure about a topic:

- Be prepared to spend more time on it. Try working through the entire question rather than just a few selected elements.

- Have a model answer available to help you in case you struggle to find the answer yourself.

You will find that practice in answering questions will restore your confidence far more effectively than just reading through notes and looking at answers to past questions.

Unit 1:
Introduction to accounting

Unit outline

Accounting is of great importance to a wide variety of individuals who have an interest in the performance of a business. Accounting information provides details of profits, the ability to pay debts and the efficient use of resources – all of which are critical to the success and survival of a business.

This unit provides an introduction to the work of bookkeepers and accountants and their roles in providing interested parties with the information they need to monitor a business's performance and make effective decisions.

Either tick these boxes to build a record of your revision, or use them to identify your strengths and weaknesses.

Your revision checklist

Specification	Theme	☺	😐	☹
1.1 The fundamentals of accounting	1.1.1 Bookkeeping and accounting			
	1.1.2 The accounting equation			

You will need to know how to:

- explain the difference between bookkeeping and accounting
- state the purposes of measuring business profit and loss
- explain the role of accounting in providing information for monitoring progress and decision making.

1.1.1 Bookkeeping and accounting

Many bookkeepers work as employees of organizations in their finance departments, but it is also possible to work for specialist firms which provide bookkeeping services for local businesses, or to be a self-employed bookkeeper working from home. More experienced bookkeepers sometimes take on some of the responsibilities of an accountant.

	Description	Examples of activities undertaken
Bookkeeping	Recording financial transactions in a systematic way, so that the owner(s) of a business can be provided with the information they need.	Bookkeepers are responsible for: • preparing accounts by entering and posting transactions • balancing accounts • preparing trial balances • verifying records and preparing reconciliation statements • storing documentation • payroll records • inventory records.
Accounting	Selecting, classifying and summarizing information in the form of financial statements, so the owner(s) of a business can manage the business more effectively.	Accountants are responsible for: • preparing financial statements which conform to legal requirements • preparing reviews and budgets • supervising the work of bookkeeping staff and offering support and advice • working with auditors (internal and external) • analysing financial statements, making recommendations and providing advice on how to improve performance • preparing tax assessments • managing and developing financial systems and budgets.

Accountants can work in private practice and provide their services for local organizations, or they can work as employees with an organization, often occupying important positions within the management team.

The importance of measuring business profit and loss

Businesses exist to make a profit and provide a return on the investments made by their owners.

In order to assess performance, an income statement is prepared annually. The income statement will detail revenues and expenses and conclude with an overall figure for profit or loss.

If a business is making a profit, the owner(s) will feel rewarded for the risk they have taken in investing in the business. The owner(s) may feel justified in expanding the business – perhaps opening new branches or expanding the products or services offered.

If a business is making a loss, the owner(s) will wish to take measures to ensure performance is improved. It will be necessary to reduce expenses, increase income or both. If a business persistently makes a loss it is in danger of closing down.

The role of accounting in providing information for monitoring progress and for decision making

Accounting processes result in the production of financial statements. Financial statements include the income statement (described above) and a statement of financial position, which sets out details about a business's resources and how these have been financed at a particular date.

These statements can be compared with those from previous years to see what progress, if any, has been made. They can also be compared with similar businesses to establish whether competitors are performing better or worse in specific areas of interest.

The financial statements are likely to be studied carefully by business owner(s), managers and other interested parties (where access is available). The analysis is likely to focus on profitability and liquidity (the ability to meet financial obligations when due) because businesses are in danger of failing if either of these key features are showing signs of weakness.

The analysis of financial statements can provide important evidence to support decisions affecting the performance of a business. These include whether or not to:

- expand
- seek ways of increasing sales
- borrow additional finance
- find ways of cutting costs
- hire additional staff.

Exam tip

There is more about the preparation of financial statements in Unit 5 and about the analysis of financial statements in Unit 6.

 Recap

1. Bookkeeping is about the detailed recording of financial transactions.

2. Accounting is about using these records to prepare financial statements to inform the owner(s) of a business of the details they need to know to monitor performance and make decisions.

3. Assessing profit or loss is a priority for any a business. Key decisions affecting the future of the business depend on these figures.

 Apply

1. Daniel is considering a career as a self-employed bookkeeper. Explain what his work will entail.

2. Kate is considering becoming qualified as an accountant and hopes to work in a large international company.

   (a) Describe what Kate's work will entail.

   (b) Explain the value of accounting to the owner of a business.

 Review

There are more details about bookkeeping and accounting in section 1.1 of *Essential Accounting for Cambridge IGCSE® & O Level (third edition)*, pages 1–2.

1.1.2 The accounting equation

The starting point for all studies of accounting is the **accounting equation**. This rule states that business resources are financed by the owner of the business and other external sources.

Assets = Owner's equity + Liabilities

Assets	Liabilities
Property, premises, land and buildings	Mortgages
Machinery	Loans
Equipment	**Trade payables**
Motor vehicles	Bank overdraft
Furniture, fixtures and fittings	
Inventory (goods for resale)	
Trade receivables	
Cash at bank	
Cash in hand	

Applying the accounting equation

The formula always holds true, so if any two elements are known, the remaining element can be calculated.

Use the information in the table below with the accounting equation to calculate the table's missing figures.

Calculating	Assets $	Owner's equity (capital) $	Liabilities $	Answer $
Owner's equity (capital)	80 000	?	20 000	60 000
Liabilities	120 000	105 000	?	15 000
Assets	?	280 000	60 000	340 000

 Recap

1. The formula which links the value of a business's assets, liabilities and owner's equity (capital) is called the accounting equation.

2. The formula states that total assets will always equal the owner's equity (capital) and liabilities.

Apply

3. Mohamed owns a restaurant; his friend Salah owns a car repair business. Identify three assets which Mohamed's business will own and which will not be owned by Salah's business.

4. Salah's assets total $162 000. He owes $11 000 to suppliers and has a bank overdraft of $4,300. Calculate the owner's equity.

Review

There are more details about the accounting equation in section 1.3 of *Essential Accounting for Cambridge IGCSE® & O Level (third edition)*, pages 3–4.

Exam-style questions

1. **(a)** Identify **four** assets which are likely to be owned by a market stallholder. **(4)**

    (b) Describe the work of an accountant. **(2)**

    (c) Explain why knowing a business's profit or loss will be important to its owner. **(2)**

    (d) Define the term 'liability'. **(1)**

2. Bilal owns a fitness centre. He has provided the following details about his business's assets and liabilities at 1 January 2019.

	$
Amounts owed to the business by members of the fitness centre	4 480
Amounts by the business to suppliers of fitness equipment	7 200
Cash in hand	850
Bank overdraft	470
Fitness equipment	38 300
Furniture and fittings	7 250
Loan from TX Finance	8 400
Premises	94 000

Calculate the business's:

(a) total assets **(1)**

(b) total liabilities **(1)**

(c) owner's equity. **(1)**

(Total marks: 12)

Before you answer the question

You will see that a variety of different keywords are used in each task: *identify*, *describe*, *define*, *calculate*, etc. It is important to understand what is required in each case.

When a task starts with the words *identify* or *state*, only a brief answer is required, quite often just one word.

Where the task is to *describe*, a more lengthy answer is required. Provide a full sentence or two so that you demonstrate a good understanding of the topic.

Where the task is to *explain*, it is important to provide some development in your answer, again to demonstrate that you understand the topic. Write in full sentences and provide development by giving examples.

Where the task is to *define*, you will be expected to give a very precise answer. Only an exact statement will be acceptable.

Where you are asked to *calculate*, it is usually important to provide some detailed workings to support your answer.

Check your answer

1. **(a)** Answers could include: market stall, inventory (goods available for sale), equipment (cash register), motor vehicle and cash in hand. **(4)**

(b) An accountant is responsible for preparing financial statements based on selecting, classifying and summarizing financial information **(1)** to benefit the owner(s) of a business and other interested parties in assessing business performance and making decisions **(1)**.

(c) Knowledge of a business's profit will enable an owner to compare current performance with previous years and with other similar businesses **(1)**. These comparisons will provide evidence to assist in future planning and decision making **(1)**.

(d) Liability is an amount owed by a business to other external parties. **(1)**

2. **(a)**

	$
Amounts owed to the business by members of the fitness centre	4 480
Cash in hand	850
Fitness equipment	38 300
Furniture and fittings	7 250
Premises	94 000
Total	144 880

(1)

(b)

	$
Amounts owed by the business to suppliers of fitness equipment	7 200
Bank overdraft	470
Loan from TX Finance	8 400
Total	16 070

(1)

(c) Owner's equity is $144 880 less $16 070, i.e. $128 810. **(1)**

⊗ Common errors

Remember to:

- consider the length of your answer – sometimes only one or two words are required
- provide a sufficiently detailed response to earn two marks
- develop your answer, providing further information to demonstrate understanding
- provide a precise answer – don't be too vague.

Multiple choice questions

1. Which one of the following would you expect to be included in the duties of a bookkeeper? **(1)**

   A analysing financial statements

   B balancing accounts

   C preparing budgets

   D working with auditors

2. Which one of the following is unlikely to be included in the duties of a bookkeeper? **(1)**

   A payroll records

   B posting transactions to ledger accounts

   C preparing tax assessments

   D verifying accounting records

3. A business has assets of $50 000 and the owner's equity is $30 000. How much are the business's liabilities? **(1)**

   A $20 000

   B $30 000

   C $50 000

   D $80 000   **(Total marks: 3)**

Structured questions

1. Javeria owns Best Office Training. Her business provides training in a wide range of business skills. Javeria employs a bookkeeper and an accountant.

   (a) Identify two responsibilities you would expect each of the following people to undertake:

   i. the bookkeeper

   ii. the accountant.   **(4)**

   At 31 December 2018 the business had the following assets, liabilities and owner's equity:

	$
Amount owing for wages	820
Bank loan	6 500
Business premises	89 300
Cash at bank	3 190
Capital	91 200
Fees owing to the business by clients	9 890
Furniture and equipment	17 860
Mortgage	?

   (b) Calculate the business's:

   i. total assets

   ii. value of the mortgage at 31 December 2018.   **(3)**

2. Htay owns a hotel. The business made a loss during the year ending 30 September 2018.

   (a) Explain why it is important that Htay is aware of the loss made by his business. (2)

   At 30 September 2018 the following details were available about the business's assets, liabilities and owner's equity:

	$
Amounts due from guests	3 580
Bank overdraft	1 130
Capital	225 000
Equipment	23 480
Furniture and fittings	19 400
General expenses due but unpaid	390
Hotel premises	185 000
Inventory	?
Loan from QXT Finance	15 300
Petty cash in hand	60
Trade payables	3 990

   (b) Calculate the business's:

       i.   total liabilities

       ii. value of inventory at 30 September 2018. (3)

   (Total marks: 12)

Unit 2:
Sources and recording of data

Unit outline

A business's daily financial activity consists of a wide variety of transactions where goods or services are bought and sold, payments are made, money is received, etc. Every transaction has an impact on a business's financial structure, sometimes changing the value of its resources, the way it is financed or its overall value. It is, therefore, vital that every transaction is carefully recorded so that accurate and up-to-date information can be provided to those who need it.

This unit introduces the double-entry system of bookkeeping, which is used to record transactions.

Either tick these boxes to build a record of your revision, or use them to identify your strengths and weaknesses.

Your revision checklist

Specification	Theme	☺	😐	☹
2.1 The double-entry system of bookkeeping	2.1.1 The double-entry system of bookkeeping – an outline			
	2.1.2 Balancing and closing accounts			
2.2 Business documents and books of prime entry	2.2.1 Business documents			
	2.2.2 Books of prime entry			

**You will
need to
know
how to:**

- outline the double-entry system of bookkeeping
- process accounting data using the double-entry system
- prepare ledger accounts
- post transactions to the ledger accounts
- balance ledger accounts as required and make transfers to financial statements
- interpret ledger accounts and their balances
- recognize the division of the ledger into the sales ledger, the purchases ledger and the nominal (general) ledger.

2.1.1 The double-entry system of bookkeeping – an outline

The system used for recording transactions is based on the following ideas:

1. There should be a separate record (i.e. account) for each aspect of any transaction.

2. Any transaction will affect two accounts.

Examples of separate accounts				
Asset	**Liability**	**Capital**	**Expense**	**Income**
Premises	Bank loan	Capital	Administration expenses	Interest received
Motor vehicles	Bank overdraft	Drawings	Advertising	Rent received
Furniture	Trade payables		Bank loan interest	Sales (of goods or services)
Fittings			Carriage inwards	
Equipment			Carriage outwards	
Inventory			Electricity	
Trade receivables			General expenses	
Cash at bank			Insurance	
Cash in hand			Office expenses	
Petty cash			Maintenance and repairs	
			Purchases (goods for sale)	
			Rent	
			Salaries	
			Selling expenses	
			Wages	

The idea that transactions always affect two accounts

In every transaction, one account receives, and the other account gives.

Transaction	Account which receives	Account which gives
Purchased some furniture by cheque	**Furniture**, as additional furniture is acquired	**Bank**, as money is given to purchase furniture
Took out a bank loan	**Bank**, as money is received as a result of taking out the loan	**Bank loan**, as bank lends the business money
Owner invested additional funds in business	**Cash/bank**, as money is received from the owner	**Capital**, as owner gives funds to the business
Purchased equipment on credit	**Equipment**, as additional equipment is acquired	**Supplier**, as supplier has provided equipment
Sold goods on credit	**Trade receivable**, as customer receives goods	**Sales**, as business sells goods to customer
Credit customer paid for goods by cheque	**Bank**, money received from customer	**Trade receivable**, customer gives money
Purchased goods on credit	**Purchases**, as goods are received	**Trade payable**, as supplier provides goods
Paid supplier by cheque	**Trade payable**, supplier receives money	**Bank**, money is given to supplier
Paid wages in cash	**Wages**, as employees receive cash	**Cash**, as money is given to employees
Owner withdrew cash for private use	**Drawings**, as owner receives money	**Cash**, as money is given to owner

How an account works

1. Each account has two sides:

    -   the left-hand side is called the debit side (abbreviated as Dr)

    -   the right-hand side is called the credit side (abbreviated as Cr).

2. An entry is required:

    -   on the **debit** side when an account **receives**

    -   on the **credit** side when an account **gives**.

3. Each side of an account has space to record:

    -   the date (month and day)

    -   a narrative

    -   the amount.

Below is an example of how the headings of an account should be presented:

Dr				Name of account			Cr
Date				Date			
Month	Day	Narrative	Amount	Month	Day	Narrative	Amount
			$				$

When there is a change in the year, it is important to record details of the year in the date column on both sides of the account.

The basic rule for narratives is to name the other account concerned in the transaction (or the source of the information, i.e. the book of prime entry).

> **Exam tip**
>
> Spend some time getting used to recording date and narrative details correctly in accounts. This is often done poorly in exams and can result in the loss of marks.

> **Exam tip**
>
> There is more about books of prime entry in section 2.2.

Posting transactions to the ledger accounts

For any transaction it is important to be able to state precisely which account will be debited and which account credited. Recording transactions is referred to as 'posting'.

Here are some typical transactions with a description of the entries to be made:

> **Exam tip**
>
> There is more about owners taking goods for own use (as in transaction J) in Unit 5.

Transaction	Details	Debit (Receiving)	Credit (Giving)
A	A sole trader started a business by investing $80 000 from private resources	Bank $80 000	Capital $80 000
B	Purchased motor vehicle by cheque $24 000	Motor vehicle $24 000	Bank $24 000
C	Took on bank loan $10 000	Bank $10 000	Bank loan $10 000
D	Purchased goods for resale on credit from X $8 000	Purchases $8 000	Trade payable X $8 000
E	Sold goods on credit $5 000 to Z	Trade receivable Z $5 000	Sales $5 000
F	Returned goods to supplier X $500	Trade payable X $500	Purchases returns $500
G	Paid general expenses by cheque $2 000	General expenses $2 000	Bank $ 2 000
H	Owner withdrew cheque for private use $1 000	Drawings $1 000	Bank $1 000
I	Credit customer Z returned goods $400	Sales returns $400	Trade receivable Z $400
J	Owner withdrew goods for own use	Drawings $2 000	Purchases $2 000

Preparing ledger accounts

Here are the ledger accounts recording transactions A–J. Dates in January 2019 have been added by way of example. To make it easier to trace the entries, the accounts are shown in alphabetic order and the narrative column also includes the relevant letter to help identify the transaction.

				NOMINAL LEDGER				
Dr			**Bank account**					**Cr**
2019				$	2019			$
Jan	2	Capital **A**		80 000	Jan	3	Motor vehicle **B**	24 000
	5	Bank loan **C**		10 000		18	General expenses **G**	2 000
						22	Drawings **H**	1 000
Dr			**Bank loan account**					**Cr**
				$	2019			$
					Jan	5	Bank **C**	10 000
Dr			**Capital account**					**Cr**
				$	2019			$
					Jan	2	Bank **A**	80 000
Dr			**Drawings account**					**Cr**
2019				$				$
Jan	22	Bank **H**		1 000				
	29	Purchases **J**		2 000				
Dr			**General expenses account**					**Cr**
2019				$				$
Jan	18	Bank **G**		2 000				
Dr			**Purchases account**					**Cr**
2019				$	2019			$
Jan	8	Trade payable X **D**		8 000	Jan	29	Drawings **J**	2 000
Dr			**Purchases returns account**					**Cr**
				$	2019			$
					Jan	14	Trade payable X **F**	500
Dr			**Sales account**					**Cr**
				$	2019			$
					Jan	12	Trade receivable Z **E**	5 000
Dr			**Sales returns account**					**Cr**
2019				$				$
Jan	25	Trade receivable Z **I**		400				
Dr			**Motor vehicles account**					**Cr**
2019				$				$
Jan	4	Bank **B**		24 000				
				PURCHASES LEDGER				
Dr			**Trade payable X**					**Cr**
2019				$	2019			$
Jan	14	Purchases returns **F**		500	Jan	8	Purchases **D**	8 000
				SALES LEDGER				
Dr			**Trade receivable Z**					**Cr**
2019				$	2019			$
Jan	12	Sales **E**		5 000	Jan	25	Sales returns **I**	400

Note: the bank account is usually extracted from the nominal ledger and shown with the cash account in the cash book (see section 3.2).

Recap

1. Transactions are recorded in ledger accounts.

2. There are separate ledger accounts for each aspect of a transaction.

3. Double-entry bookkeeping is based on the idea that every transaction will affect two accounts: one account will receive value and the other account will give value.

4. The account receiving value is debited, i.e. an entry is made on the left-hand side of the account.

5. The account giving value is credited, i.e. an entry is made on the right-hand side of the account.

6. There are strict rules about how dates and narratives are recorded when making entries in ledger account.

Exam tip

It is a common error to include the purchases account in the purchases ledger (rather than the nominal ledger) and the sales account in the sales ledger (rather than the nominal ledger). Only personal accounts are recorded in the purchases and sales ledgers.

Apply

1. The following transactions occurred when Vikash opened his business:

    i. paid $40 000 into a business bank account as capital to start the business

    ii. purchased equipment worth $21 000 by cheque

    iii. purchased goods for resale on credit from supplier TX Stores, $11 000

    iv. withdrew a cheque for $200 for private use

    v. sold goods on credit to JK Retail, $3,600

    vi. returned goods to TX Stores, $300 because they were not as ordered

    vii. had to take back some goods he had sold to JK Retail on credit, for $200, because they were damaged

    viii. paid TX Stores $7,000 by cheque

    ix. received a cheque from JK Retail for $1,900 in part settlement of the amount due.

    For each transaction, state which account will be debited and which account will be credited.

Review

There are more details about the double-entry system of recording transactions in sections 2.3–2.5 of *Essential Accounting for Cambridge IGCSE® & O Level (third edition)*, pages 20–32.

2.1.2 Balancing and closing accounts

At the end of a financial period all ledger accounts should be either:

- balanced – where there is an amount left in the account, or
- closed – where there is no balance (often because the amount left in the account has been transferred elsewhere in the accounting system).

Balancing an asset account	The account before balancing					
	Dr			Cash account		Cr
	2018		$	2018		$
	May 1	Balance	180	May 11	Drawings	50
				19	Wages	110

Step 1: Record the balance on the side with the lower value; use the narrative 'Balance c/d' (avoid using abbreviations if possible).

Dr			Cash account		Cr
2018		$	2018		$
May 1	Balance	180	May 11	Drawings	50
			19	Wages	110
			31	**Balance c/d**	**20**

Step 2: Record totals on each side of the account on the same horizontal line.

Dr			Cash account		Cr
2018		$	2018		$
May 1	Balance	180	May 11	Drawings	50
			19	Wages	110
			31	Balance c/d	20
		180			**180**

Step 3: Make a matching entry for the balance c/d – in other words debit the account with the balance b/d.

Dr			Cash account		Cr
2018		$	2018		$
May 1	Balance	180	May 11	Drawings	50
			19	Wages	110
			31	Balance c/d	20
		180			180
June 1	**Balance b/d**	**20**			

The balance is brought down to first day of the next month.

Balancing a liability account	Here is a balanced liability account. Steps 1–3 are indicated by the numbers **1–3**.					
	Dr			Trade payable: TLX Wholesalers		Cr
	2019		$	2019		$
	Jan 20	Bank	3 000	Jan 1	Balance b/d	1 480
	31	Balance c/d **1**	3 080	11	Purchases	4 600
		2	6 080		**2**	6 080
				Feb 1	Balance b/d **3**	20

Closing accounts	Where the account has several entries on either side, close the account by recording a total on the same horizontal line.

General expenses account

Dr				Cr
2018		$	2018	$
June 30	Bank	2 400	Dec 31 Income statement	5 180
Oct 12	Bank	1 960		
Dec 14	Bank	820		
		5 180		**5 180**

Where the account has just one entry on each side, close the account with a single total line on each side of the account.

Drawings account

Dr				Cr
2018		$	2018	$
Sept 30	Bank	8 300	Dec 31 Capital	8 300

Interpreting accounts and their balances

Interpreting an account means explaining what the account shows. It is necessary to look at each transaction and give a detailed description of what has happened.

Here is the account of a credit customer in a business's sales ledger:

Trade receivable: BZ Retail Stores

Dr		$			Cr
2018		$	2018		$
Nov 1	Balance	2 400	Nov 4	Bank	2 280
19	Sales	5 200	4	Discounts allowed	120
			23	Sales returns	150
			30	Balance c/d	5 050
		7 600			7 600
Dec 1	Balance b/d	5 050			

Exam tip

The balancing process is often a noticeable weakness in exam answers. It is worthwhile making sure you practise the techniques shown above.

Here are two interpretations of the account: one is unsatisfactory, because it lacks detail; the other is much better, with attention paid to giving precise information.

	Not done well	Better answer
Nov 1	The account has a balance of $2 400	The customer owed $2 400
4	The customer paid the amount due less a cash discount	The customer settled the amount due. The amount paid by cheque was $2 280. The customer deducted a 5% cash discount of $120
19	Goods were sold	The customer was sold goods on credit, $5 200
23	The customer returned goods	The customer returned goods, $150
30	The account had a balance of $5 050	The customer owed $5 050

⏪ Recap

1. Accounts are either balanced or closed at regular intervals, and always at the end of a financial period.

2. There are different techniques for balancing accounts and for closing accounts.

3. When balancing accounts, the terms 'balance c/d' (before the account totals) and 'balance b/d' (after the account totals) are used.

4. It is important to be able to provide detailed descriptions of what each entry in a ledger account means.

✏ Apply

2. The following transactions were recorded in a business's bank account in 2019. Jan 1 balance of cash at bank $2,700; Jan 9 paid salaries $980; Jan 17 cash sales banked $1,810; Jan 23 withdrew cheque for $540 for private use. Prepare and balance the account on 31 January.

3. The following transactions were recorded in a business's bank loan account in 2018: June 1 borrowed $8,000 from the bank (funds were transferred to the business bank account); Oct 1 repaid $800 of the loan by cheque. Prepare the bank loan account and balance it on 31 December.

4. A business's nominal ledger includes the following accounts and entries for December 2018:

   i. insurance: Dec 1 opening debit balance $1,820; Dec 15 cheque paid for insurance $270; Dec 31 balance of account transferred to the income statement

   ii. drawings: Dec 1 opening debit balance $14 910, Dec 21 goods taken for own use $360, Dec 31 balance of account transferred to the capital account.

   Prepare the ledger accounts and close them on 31 December 2018.

⏱ Review

There is more about balancing and closing accounts in sections 2.10 and 2.11 of *Essential Accounting for Cambridge IGCSE® & O Level (third edition)*, pages 50–9.

- recognize and understand the following business documents: invoice, credit note, debit note, statement of account, cheque, receipt
- complete pro-forma business documents
- explain the use of the following business documents: invoice, credit, note, cheque counterfoil, paying-in slip, receipt, bank statement
- explain the advantage of using various books of prime entry
- explain and process accounting data in the books of prime entry: cash book, petty cash book, sales journal, purchases, journal, sales returns journal, purchases returns journal and the general journal
- distinguish between and account for trade and cash discounts.

2.2.1 Business documents

Document	Description and details to be recorded on documents
Invoice	• Used when goods are supplied on credit • Details included: name and address of supplier; name and address of customer; date; details of goods being sold, prices and total amount to be paid • Prices quoted could be reduced by a trade discount (see below) • Invoice could indicate that a cash discount (see below) is available for prompt payment It is useful to refer to a 'purchases invoice' (for goods which have been purchased on credit) or to a 'sales invoice' (for goods sold on credit)
Credit note	• Used when goods are returned (because they are damaged, faulty, not as ordered or overcharged) • Details included: information about supplier and customer, date, details of goods being returned, prices and total value of returns If trade discount was deducted from the value of goods originally supplied, then trade discount must also be deducted from the value of goods being returned.
Debit note	• Used to inform the supplier of goods of any overcharges shown on an invoice or details of goods being returned • Details included: information about supplier and customer; reference to the original invoice, information about goods being returned or overcharges Debit notes do not lead directly to entries being made in accounting records.
Statement of account	• Issued to each credit customer, usually at monthly intervals • Summarizes the transactions which have occurred during the month, e.g. goods supplied, returns, payments received from the customer, cash discounts allowed • Highlights the amount outstanding at the end of the month, and so acts as a reminder of the amount to be paid • Can be used by customers to check there are no errors in their own records or those of the supplier Statements of account do not lead to entries being made in accounting records, as all the information shown will already have been recorded.
Cheque	• Used to make payments to another person or organization from a bank account • Details included: date, payee (the person or organization being paid), the amount in words, the amount in figures, signature of the individual responsible for making the payment Cheques are detached from a counterfoil (or stub) on which the date, payee and amount are recorded. This counterfoil is used to make entries for the payments in the cash book.
Receipt	• Used to acknowledge that money has been received by cheque or in cash in payment for goods or services • Details included: date, name of business or person who has paid, the amount paid Receipts are often issued by cash registers when payment is made.

Exam tip

It is easy to forget to deduct trade discount when preparing a credit note when the goods involved were originally subject to a trade discount reduction.

Exam tip

Don't forget that a debit note used to inform a supplier of returns or overcharging is not used to make entries in the accounting records.

Discounts: key points

	Trade discount	Cash discount
Purpose	• Offered to businesses engaged in the same line of activity • Reward for making a large order • Not normally available to private individuals • Often a large percentage, between 20% and 33%	• Offered to encourage prompt payment by credit customers • A business's liquidity is improved if customers pay more quickly • Normally offered in the range 2–5%
Presence on paperwork	• Appears as a reduction in the value of goods supplied on an invoice and any subsequent credit note	• Invoices normally show information about the *possibility* of a cash discount as a footnote • The format used is, for example: 'terms: 5%, 30 days'
Recording	• Trade discount is not recorded in ledger accounts • Only the net amount is shown • There is no such thing as a trade discount account	• Cash discount is recorded in the double-entry system • A note is made of discounts allowed (to customers) and discounts received (from suppliers) in memorandum columns in a three-column cash book • A supplier's account is debited with discounts received • A customer's account is credited with discounts allowed

2.2.2 Books of prime entry

All entries in an accounting system are based on information provided by source documents. Source documents are carefully stored by a business because they provide evidence for all the information shown in the accounting records.

The first record of any transaction is made in a book of prime entry using information extracted from source documents. Transactions are recorded in strict date order in each book of prime entry.

Books of prime entry have several advantages:

• They make it possible to summarize information and provide totals for certain types of transaction, which reduces the number of entries in ledger accounts and therefore saves time.

• As there are seven different books of prime entry is it possible to divide the work of making a first record of transactions among a small team of accounting staff.

• They provide the information required for control accounts (see section 3.4).

Book of prime entry	Purpose	Source documents used
Purchases journal	To record purchases of goods on credit	Purchases invoice
Sales journal	To records sales of goods on credit	Sales invoice
Purchases returns journal	To record goods returned to suppliers previously purchased on credit	Credit note (received from supplier)
Sales returns journal	To record goods returned by customers previously sold on credit	Credit note (copy of credit note issued to customer)
Three-column cash book	• To record receipts and payments of cash • To record receipts and payments affecting the business's bank account • To record **contra entries** • To note discounts allowed • To note discounts received	For cash receipts: • till rolls (from cash registers detailing cash sales) • copies of cash receipts issued For cash payments: • cash receipts For bank receipts: • paying-in slip counterfoils • credit transfers For bank payments: • cheque counterfoils • bank statements
Petty cash book	To record small cash payments (below a limit set by the business) using the **imprest** system	Petty cash vouchers
General journal	To record all transactions which cannot be recorded in other books of prime entry	• Invoice for the purchase of non-current assets • Emails/memos from owner, managers, employees, other businesses

Sometimes books of prime entry are referred to as 'books of original entry' or 'subsidiary books'.

The cash book is both a book of prime entry and also part of the double-entry system. This is because it provides the first record of money transactions but also acts as ledger accounts for bank and cash.

Bank statements provide details of bank charges, direct debt payments, standing order payments, **dishonoured cheques** and electronic means of transferring money (such as credit transfers).

Journals

Purchases/Sales/Purchases returns/Sales returns journal				
Date	Customer/Supplier	Source document number	$	$
2019				
Jan 24	MK Retail	1234	3 200	
	Less 25% trade discount		800	
				2 400

The subtotals shown for each document are totalled at the end of the month (or more frequently if required) and posted to the relevant nominal account (i.e. Dr Purchases, Cr Sales, Dr Sales returns, Cr Purchases returns).

The totals should be accompanied by a narrative, e.g. Total purchases for the month. The four journals are sometimes called 'day books'.

The returns journals are sometimes referred to as 'returns inwards journals' (for sales returns) and 'returns outwards journals' (for purchases returns).

Cash book

Dr										Cr
					Cash book					
Date	Details	Discounts allowed	Cash	Bank	Date	Details	Discounts received	Cash	Bank	
		$	$	$				$	$	$

> **Exam tip**
>
> It is a common error to try to balance the discount columns in a cash book.

The discount columns are a memorandum record and not part of the double entry. They are totalled at the end of the month and the totals are posted to the 'discounts allowed' and 'discounts received' accounts in the nominal ledger.

The cash and bank columns are balanced at regular intervals. The bank balance brought down could be debit (positive bank balance) or credit (bank overdraft).The cash account can only have a debit balance.

Petty cash book

				Petty cash book				
Receipts $	Date	Details	Voucher number	Payments $	Stationery $	Postage $	Cleaning $	Purchases ledger $

The petty cash book consists of a simple cash account (starting with the receipts column and ending with the payments column) plus analysis columns (stationery, postage, cleaning and purchases ledger in the above).

Each payment is entered twice: once in the payments column and again in an appropriate analysis column.

Analysis columns provide (often monthly) totals for transfer to the nominal ledger. If there is an analysis column for purchases ledger account payments, each entry is posted separately. The total of this analysis column is not used.

The cash account element of the petty cash book is balanced in the normal way.

If the imprest system is used, the petty cashier will have a float to use to make payments. This ensures there is some control over petty cash and the responsibility given to a petty cashier. At regular intervals, the imprest is restored. The petty cashier should receive the total of the amount spent in that period.

General journal

	General journal			
Date		Details	$	$
		Account to be debited	xxx	
		Account to be credited		xxx
		Narrative		

The general journal is often referred to as 'the journal'. Transactions are recorded which cannot be recorded in any of the other books of prime entry. These include:

- purchase of non-current assets on credit
- the opening of a new set of books
- corrections of errors (see section 3.2)
- withdrawals of goods for own use
- transfers of information in one account to another account.

The account to be debited should be recorded first. The account to be credited should be recorded second (and slightly inset, as shown above). Unless otherwise stated, each entry should include a narrative which explains the reasons for the entries being made.

◀◀ Recap

1. Information about transactions is taken from source documents.

2. There are source documents to cover all forms of cash and credit transactions.

3. Source documents are retained by a business to provide documentary evidence to support every entry made in the books of account.

4. Books of prime entry are used to make the first record of transactions in the accounting system.

5. There are seven books of prime entry.

6. The cash book acts as both a book of prime entry and as ledger accounts for cash and bank.

7. Transaction details are posted from books of prime entry to ledger accounts, where appropriate totals are posted (rather than individual amounts).

8. Trade discounts are sometimes offered on large orders to businesses in the same trade. Only the net amount charged is entered in ledger accounts.

9. Cash discounts are offered to encourage prompt payment. Where an account due is settled within the specified time limit, entries are made to record any cash discount deducted in the ledger accounts.

✎ Apply

1. Padma owns a wholesale business. During the last week Padma:

    i. purchased goods on credit

    ii. banked cash sales

    iii. received information about the business's bank charges

    iv. sent a document to the credit supplier to say that some goods on credit were faulty

    v. received a document from the credit supplier stating the value of purchases returned

    vi. sold goods on credit

    vii. paid the supplier the amount due by cheque

    viii. paid for some office stationery in cash

    ix. paid for an employee's travel expenses from petty cash

    x. sent a document to a credit customer as a reminder of the amount outstanding.

For each transaction, state which document would be used to record the information.

2. The following source documents are to be used to record transactions in a business's books of account:

i.   invoice received from a supplier for goods for resale

ii. copy of credit note issued to a credit customer

iii. bank statement showing details of a direct debit payment

iv. invoice received for the purchase of a non-current asset

v.   paying-in slip counterfoil showing details of cash sales

vi. note from the owner giving details of some goods taken for own use

vii. bank statement showing details of a credit transfer from a credit customer

viii. cash receipt giving details of the amount spent on cleaning materials

ix. credit note received from a credit supplier.

For each source document, state which book of prime entry will be used to record the transaction.

Review

There are more details about source documents and books of prime entry in sections 2.12–2.26 of *Essential Accounting for Cambridge IGCSE® & O Level (third edition)*, pages 61–106.

Exam-style questions

1. The following transactions are to be recorded in a business's ledger accounts:

2018		
Oct	1	Owner paid $38 000 from private resources into a business bank account
	3	Purchased goods for resale from TJ on credit, $9 200
	7	Paid rent by cheque, $1 200
	11	Purchased motor vehicle and paid by cheque, $17 200
	15	Sold goods and banked proceeds, $4 100
	18	Sold goods on credit to KLX, $3 900
	21	Returned goods to TJ purchased on credit, $300
	28	Received cheque from KLX in full settlement of the amount due

(a) Prepare ledger accounts and record the transactions. **(16)**

(b) Balance the following accounts on 31 October 2018:

    i. bank account **(2)**

    ii. trade payable TJ **(3)**

    iii. trade receivable KLX. **(2)**

(Total marks: 23)

Before you answer the question

You might like to give each transaction a little thought: decide which accounts are involved; decide which account receives and which account gives. Don't forget that attention to detail is very important!

Check your answer

NOMINAL LEDGER						
Dr			**Bank account**			Cr
	2018		$	2018		$
Oct 1	Capital **(1)**		38 000	Oct 7	Rent **(1)**	1 200
15	Sales **(1)**		4 100	11	Motor vehicle **(1)**	17 200
28	Trade receivable KLX **(1)**		3 900			

	Dr		**Capital account**			Cr
			$	2018		$
				Oct 1	Bank **(1)**	38 000

Dr			**Purchases account**			Cr
	2018		$			$
Oct 3	Trade payable TJ **(1)**		9 200			

	Dr		**Purchases returns account**			Cr
			$	2018		$
				Oct 21	Trade payable TJ **(1)**	300

Dr			**Rent account**			Cr
	2018		$			$
Oct 7	Bank **(1)**		1 200			

	Dr		**Sales account**			Cr
			$	2018		$
				Oct 15	Bank **(1)**	4 100
				18	Trade receivable KLX **(1)**	3 900

Dr			**Motor vehicles account**			Cr
	2018		$			$
Oct 11	Bank **(1)**		17 200			

PURCHASES LEDGER						
Dr			**Trade payable TJ**			Cr
	2018		$	2018		$
Oct 21	Purchases returns **(1)**		330	Oct 3	Purchases **(1)**	9 200

SALES LEDGER						
Dr			**Trade receivable KLX**			Cr
	2018		$	2018		$
Oct 18	Sales **(1)**		3 900	Oct 18	Bank **(1)**	3 900

Note: each mark can only be awarded if the entry includes the correct date, narrative and amount, and is recorded on the correct side of the account.

(b)

i.

Dr			Bank account			Cr
2018		$	2018			$
Oct 1	Capital	38 000	Oct 7	Rent		1 200
15	Sales	4 100	11	Motor vehicle		17 200
28	Trade receivable KLX	3 900	31	Balance c/d		27 600
		46 000	**(1 totals on both sides)**			46 000
Nov 1	Balance b/d **(1)**	27 600				

ii.

Dr			Trade payable TJ		Cr
2018		$	2018		$
Oct 21	Purchases returns	330	Oct 3	Purchases **(1)**	9 200
31	Balance c/d	8 870			
		9 200	**(1 totals on both sides)**		9 200
			Nov 1	Balance b/d **(1)**	8 870

iii.

Dr			Trade receivable KLX		Cr
2018		$	2018		$
Oct 18	Sales **(1)**	3 900	Oct 18	Bank **(1)**	3 900

2. Shanaya was preparing her accounting records for November 2018. The following source documents are available:

Date		Source document	Details
Nov	3	Sales invoice	JV Wholesalers, goods list price $3 800 less 25% trade discount
	7	Cheque counterfoil	Drawings $375
	11	Till roll	Cash sales $4 380
	13	Paying-in slip counterfoil	Cash $3 900 and cheque from credit customer WQ Retail in settlement of amount due $1 600 less 5% cash discount
	17	Credit note copy	JV Wholesalers, goods list price $420 less 25% trade discount
	19	Bank statement	Bank charges $85
	22	Cash receipt	Stationery $120
	24	Purchases invoice	LX Supplies, goods for resale list price $4 200 less 20% trade discount
	27	Bank statement	Direct debit payment for electricity $320
	29	Cheque counterfoil	Payment of amount due to LX Supplies for goods supplied on 24 November, less $56 cash discount

The cash book at 1 November 2018 recorded balances of cash in hand $290 and cash at bank $830.

Prepare the books of prime entry required to record the transactions for November 2018. Balance the cash book at 30 November 2018.

(Total marks: 21)

Before you answer the question

You may like to make a note of which book of prime entry will be required for each transaction.

Some transactions require calculations of trade and cash discounts. It might be helpful to work out the figures before starting to write your answer.

Remember the importance of correctly recording dates and narratives.

Check your answer

Purchases journal			$	$	
2018					
Nov 24	LX Supplies		4 200		
	Less 20% trade discount		840		
				3 360	**(1)**
30	Total credit purchases for the month			3 360	**(1)**

Sales journal			$	$	
2018					
Nov 3	JV Wholesalers		3 800		
	Less 25% trade discount		950		
				2 850	**(1)**
30	Total credit sales for the month			2 850	**(1)**

Sales returns journal			$	$	
2018					
Nov 17	JV Wholesalers		420		
	Less 25% trade discount		105		
				315	**(1)**
30	Total sales returns for the month			315	**(1)**

⊗ Common errors

Remember to:

- include the trade discount when making an entry in the sales returns journal

- provide a total for each of the journals, and include the phrase 'for the month'

- provide an accurate narrative based on the other account affected by the transaction

- calculate the cash discounts correctly

- total the discount columns rather than balancing them

- bring the balances down for cash and bank at 1 December.

Dr					Cash book					Cr
Date	Details	Discounts allowed	Cash	Bank	Date	Details	Discounts received	Cash	Bank
2018		$	$	$	2018		$	$	$
Nov 1	Balances b/d **(1)**		290	830	Nov 7	Drawings **(1)**			375
11	Sales **(1)**		4 380		13	Bank **(1)**		3 900	
13	Cash **(1)**			3 900	19	Bank charges **(1)**			85
13	WQ Retail **(2)**	80		1 520	22	Stationery **(1)**		120	
					27	Electricity **(1)**			320
					29	LX Supplies **(1)**		56	3 304
					30	Balances c/d		650	2 166
	(1)	80	4 670	6 250		**(1)**	56	4 670	6 250
Dec 1	Balances b/d **(2)**		650	2 166					

Multiple choice questions

1. Which one of the following accounts normally has debit balance? **(1)**

   A bank loan

   B drawings

   C sales

   D trade payables

2. Which one of the following accounts normally has a credit balance? **(1)**

   A cash

   B purchases

   C returns outwards

   D trade receivables

3. Sachin owns a shoe shop. Which one of the following entries correctly records the purchase of furniture on credit from T Limited for business use? **(1)**

	Debit	Credit
A	Furniture	T Limited
B	Purchases	T Limited
C	T Limited	Furniture
D	T Limited	Purchases

4. Haroon purchased goods from Chan. Some of the goods were faulty. Which document will Haroon send to Chan requesting a refund? **(1)**

   A credit note

   B debit note

   C receipt

   D statement of account

5. A petty cash book is maintained using the imprest system with a float of $80. During a recent month the petty cashier recorded petty cash vouchers totalling $45. How much should the petty cashier receive to restore the float? (1)

A $35   C $80

B $45   D $125

6. The following is an extract from a business's cash book:

Dr											Cr
	Date	Details	Discounts	Cash	Bank	Date	Details	Discounts	Cash	Bank	
			$	$	$			$	$	$	
			240					170			

Cash book

What entries should be made in the discount accounts in the nominal ledger? (1)

	Debit	Credit
A	discounts allowed $170	discounts received $240
B	discounts allowed $240	discounts received $170
C	discounts received $170	discounts allowed $240
D	discounts received $240	discounts allowed $170

(Total marks: 6)

Structured questions

1. Khalid recently opened a business selling electrical goods. The following transactions occurred during the business's first month of trading:

2019		
Feb	1	Khalid opened the business by providing capital in the form of a motor vehicle $17 000, transferring funds to a business bank account $24 000
	3	Purchased goods on credit from KV, $7 200
	7	Paid rent by cheque $1 800
	11	Purchased goods and paid by cheque $2 100
	14	Sold goods and banked proceeds $3 200
	15	Returned goods to KV previously purchased on credit, $190
	18	Paid KV the amount due by cheque
	21	Khalid withdrew a cheque $400 and goods $200 for private use
	24	Sold goods on credit to HX $4 700
	28	HX returned goods previously sold to them on credit $320

(a) Define the term 'debit'. (1)

(b) Prepare ledger accounts and record the transactions for February 2019. (24)

2. The following accounts appeared in the books of Jasmine's business.

Dr			Bank account		Cr
2018		$	2018		$
Nov 1	Balance b/d	2 230	Nov 20	Equipment	6 450
11	Sales	4 630	27	Trade payable MZ	2 200
			30	Drawings	520

Dr			General expenses account		Cr
2018		$	2018		$
Nov 1	Balance b/d	2 230	Nov 30	Income statement	2 450
27	Cash	220			

Dr			Trade receivable JK		Cr
2018		$	2018		$
Nov 1	Balance b/d	1 940	Nov 19	Sales returns	90
13	Sales	730			

Dr			Trade payable MZ		Cr
2018		$	2018		$
Nov 27	Bank	2 200	Nov 1	Balance b/d	2 200

Dr			Sales account		Cr
2018		$	2018		$
Nov 30	Income statement	97 810	Nov 1	Balance b/d	92 450
			11	Bank	4 630
			13	Trade receivable JK	730

Copy the accounts as shown and balance or close the accounts as appropriate. (6)

3. Krishna owns a sportswear shop. During January 2019 the following source documents were to be recorded in his business's books of account:

Jan	3	Purchases invoice	Kabir Wholesalers goods list price $5 400 less 33⅓% trade discount
	5	Sales invoice	Sai Sports Centre goods list price $1 400 less 20% trade discount
	8	Credit note	Kabir Wholesalers goods list price $210 purchased on 3 January
	11	Purchase invoice	M Limited goods list price $4 400 less 25% trade discount
	14	Copy of credit note	Sai Sports Centre goods list price $80 sold on 5 January
	18	Sales invoice	Kyra goods $580
	21	Paying-in slip counterfoil	Kyra in full settlement of the balance due on 1 January 2019 less 2.5% cash discount
	27	Cheque counterfoil	Kabir Wholesalers in full settlement of amount outstanding on this date less 5% cash discount

On 1 January 2019 the following balances appeared in the business's purchases and sales ledgers:

- purchases ledger: Kabir Wholesalers $3 200

                        M Limited $1 820

- sales ledger: Kyra $640

(a) Explain the difference between trade discount and cash discount.   **(4)**

(b) Prepare the following books of prime entry:

    i.   purchases journal   **(3)**

    ii. sales journal   **(3)**

    iii. purchases returns journal   **(2)**

    iv. sales returns journal.   **(2)**

(c) Prepare the following ledger accounts:

    i.   Kabir Wholesalers   **(6)**

    ii. M Limited   **(4)**

    iii. Sai Sports Centre   **(5)**

    iv. Kyra.   **(3)**

The accounts should be balanced or closed on 31 January 2019.

4. The following transactions are to be recorded in a business's general journal:

2019		
Feb	1	A new set of books was opened to record the following: cash at bank $4 800, motor vehicle $18 500, inventory $14 200, bank loan $6 000 and capital
	4	Purchased equipment for business use on credit from JK Supplies, $3 900
	14	The owner withdrew goods for private use $190
	28	Corrected an error in the accounts: motor vehicle repairs $220 had been debited to the motor vehicles account

(a) Prepare the business's general journal for February 2019.   **(13)**

The business also maintains a petty cash book.

(b) Describe two advantages of using a petty cash book.   **(2)**

(Total marks: 78)

Unit 3:
Verification of accounting records

Unit outline

Accounting information is used to judge the performance of a business and informs important decisions which affect the future of the organization.

However, accounting information can only be useful if it is accurate. If there are errors in the accounting records, decision makers could lose confidence in financial statements and, even worse, make misguided decisions.

To ensure accounting records are accurate and reliable, various techniques are used to check aspects of the accounting system. These techniques are the subject of this unit.

Either tick these boxes to build a record of your revision, or use them to identify your strengths and weaknesses.

Your revision checklist

Specification	Theme	☺	😐	☹
3.1 The trial balance	3.1.1 Uses and limitations of a trial balance; preparing a trial balance			
	3.1.2 Errors not revealed by a trial balance			
3.2 Correction of errors	3.2.1 Types of error and their correction			
	3.2.2 The suspense account			
	3.2.3 Correcting financial statements			
3.3 Bank reconciliation	3.3.1 Bank statements			
	3.3.2 Updating cash books			
	3.3.3 Bank reconciliation statements			
3.4 Control accounts	3.4.1 The role and use of control accounts			
	3.4.2 Control account formats			

- explain that a trial balance is a statement of ledger balances on a particular date
- outline the uses and limitations of a trial balance
- prepare a trial balance from a given list of balances and amend a trial balance which contains errors
- identify and explain errors which do not affect the trial balance.

3.1.1 Uses and limitations of a trial balance; preparing a trial balance

The trial balance is a list of all the balances in an accounting system on a particular date. It has separate columns to record the debit balances and the credit balances.

Uses	Limitations
Helps check the accuracy of the accounting records. It is an arithmetical check: the totals of the debit balances should equal the total of the credit balances. If the totals do not agree there must be errors in the double entry.	Does not reveal every type of error. There can still be errors even if the totals agree (e.g. if an entire transaction was omitted from the accounts).
Helps with the preparation of financial statements, since all the required details are summarized in one list.	

Preparing a trial balance

Here is a summary of how the various types of account are recorded in a trial balance:

Debit balances	Credit balances
Assets	Liabilities
Drawings	Capital
Expenses	Revenue
Returns inwards	Other income (e.g. rent received)
Suspense account*	Provisions (e.g. for depreciation)
	Returns outwards
	Suspense account*

* See section 3.2 for more details of suspense accounts.

Some points to check are as follows:

- Assuming end-of-year financial statements have not been prepared, the opening inventory appears in a trial balance. The closing inventory will be given as additional information.

- Returns are sometimes incorrectly recorded on a trial balance. It can be helpful to remember that returns *to* a business are the opposite of revenue, and so are shown as debit entries. Returns *from* a business are the opposite of purchases, and so are shown as credit entries.

- A trial balance should have a full title, e.g. Trial balance at 31 August 2018.

✎ **Apply**

1. A business's trial balance includes the following:

Total assets	$72 000
Total liabilities	$14 000
Total expenses	$24 000
Purchases	$64 000
Revenue	$105 000
Drawings	$9 000
Returns inwards	$3 000
Returns outwards	$5 000

The trial balance totals agreed when the balance of the capital account was included. What was the balance of the capital account?

2. On which side of a trial balance should you record the following account balances?

   (a) carriage inwards

   (b) discounts allowed

   (c) discounts received

   (d) returns inwards

   (e) returns outwards.

◀◀ **Recap**

1. A trial balance checks the accuracy of the accounting records, but it cannot reveal every possible error.

2. The main categories of accounts with debit balances are assets, expenses and drawings.

3. The main categories of accounts with credit balances are liabilities, capital and income.

⏱ **Review**

There are more details about how to prepare a trial balance in *Essential Accounting for Cambridge IGCSE® & O Level (third edition)*, in section 2.6, pages 33–4.

3.1.2 Errors not revealed by a trial balance

Error	Description
Commission	An entry has been made in the wrong account within the same class of account. The entry is for the correct amount and on the correct side.
Compensating	Where, by coincidence, two or more unconnected errors cancel each other out.
Complete reversal	Both entries for a transaction are recorded on the wrong sides. The entries are in the correct accounts and for the correct amounts.
Omission	An entire transaction has been omitted from the accounting records.
Original entry	An incorrect figure has been entered in the accounts. The entries are on the correct sides and in the correct accounts.
Principle	An entry has been made in the wrong account and in the wrong class of account. The entry is for the correct amount and on the correct side.

Here are some points to note:

- The errors are corrected by means of journal entries.

- An error of reversal is corrected by entering twice the amount of the error.

✏ Apply

3. A bookkeeper made the following errors:

   i. An invoice received for $320 was recorded in the purchases journal as $230.

   ii. The cost of repairing a motor vehicle, $560, was debited to the motor vehicles account.

   iii. A cheque from a credit customer, $320, was debited in the customer's account and credited in the bank account.

   Identify the type of error made in **i**, **ii** and **iii**.

4. The following errors were discovered in a business's books of account:

   i. The payment of wages ($980) has been credited in the cash book, but no entry has been made in the wages account. At the same time, the balance of a trade payable's account was understated by $980.

   ii. A credit note for $148 received from a credit supplier was overlooked.

   iii. A cheque in payments of carriage inwards (for $140) was debited to the carriage outwards account.

   Identify the type of error made in **i**, **ii** and **iii**.

⏱ Review

For more details and examples of the types of error not revealed by a trial balance, see *Essential Accounting for Cambridge IGCSE® & O Level (third edition)*, sections 3.1 and 3.2, pages 114–17.

You will need to know how to:

- correct errors by means of journal entries
- explain the use of a suspense account as a temporary measure to correct the trial balance
- correct errors by means of suspense accounts
- adjust a profit or loss for an accounting period after the correction of errors
- correct errors in a statement of financial position.

3.2.1 Types of error and their correction

In section 3.1.2, we saw the types of error which cannot be revealed by the trial balance. In each case, these errors can be corrected by making a journal entry.

The journal entry will require a matching debit entry and credit entry in the accounts involved. The suspense account is not affected by the error correction.

Errors revealed by the trial balance

Type of error	Description	Example	How corrected
Transposition	One figure is correct; the matching figure is incorrect.	Wages paid in cash: $332 Dr entry wages $332; Cr entry cash $323	Dr Suspense $99 Cr Cash $99
Addition	A miscalculation is made.	Miscalculation of total of purchases journal ($430); the correct total was $450.	Dr Purchases $20 Cr Suspense $20
	The balance of an account is overstated or understated.	Trade receivable account balance b/d was $1200; the correct figure was $1150.	Dr Suspense $50 Cr Trade receivable $50
Posting	The total of the sales journal is posted incorrectly.	The total of the sales journal was posted as $980; the correct figure was $930.	Dr Sales $50 Cr Suspense $50
Unequal posting	The amount of the debit entry does not equal the credit entry.	Purchase of a non-current asset on credit ($1100) was entered correctly in the asset account, but was credited to the payable's account as $1000.	Dr Suspense $100 Cr Payable $100
Partial omission	Either the debit or credit entry is not recorded.	The total of the 'discounts allowed' column in the cash book ($112) was not posted to the nominal ledger.	Dr Discount allowed $112 Cr Suspense $112

Recap

1. There are six errors which do not affect the agreement of the trial balance totals.

2. Some errors result in an unequal double entry (i.e. the debit and credit entry figures do not match) and this results in the trial balance totals not agreeing.

3. All errors are corrected by means of journal entries.

4. Errors which affect the agreement of the trial balance totals result in a correction being made in the suspense account.

Apply

1. Identify whether each of the following errors would affect agreement of the trial balance totals:

    i.   A cheque received from a credit customer for $167 was recorded in the accounts as Dr Bank $176; Cr Trade receivable $176.

    ii. The total of the discounts allowed column in the cash book $312 was debited to the discounts allowed account as $321.

    iii. The entries made for some goods taken for own use by the owner were Dr Drawings $160; Cr Inventory $160.

    iv. The balance of the returns outwards account was overstated by $100.

2. Referring to the errors in the question above, calculate the difference in the trial balance totals.

Review

There are some more illustrations of errors which affect the agreement of the trial balance totals in section 3.3 of *Essential Accounting for Cambridge IGCSE® & O Level (third edition)*, pages 118–20.

3.2.2 The suspense account

When the totals of a trial balance do not agree, an entry is made in the column with the lower total figure for the difference and labelled '**suspense account**'. The suspense account entry, which could be in the debit or credit column, ensures the trial balance columns agree. The suspense account is shown in the nominal ledger.

When all the errors have been discovered and corrected, the suspense account will no longer be required and so will be closed.

Recap

1. A suspense account is used to make the totals of a trial balance agree.

2. The entry could be on the debit or credit side of the trial balance – whichever is lower.

3. A suspense account is opened in the nominal ledger and the opening balance is recorded on the same side as the entry in the trial balance.

4. The suspense account will be closed when all the errors affecting the trial balance totals are found and corrected.

Apply

3. The debit column of a trial balance totalled $187 362 and the credit column totalled $194 276. State what entry should be made in the suspense account as a result of the disagreement in the trial balance totals.

4. A suspense account has an opening balance of Dr $360. The following errors were discovered and the trial balance totals agreed:

   i. The total of the returns inwards journal ($170) had not been posted to the nominal ledger account.

   ii. The balance of the discounts received account had been understated by $70.

   iii. Cash drawings of $280 had not been posted from the cash book.

   iv. The balance of the petty cash book had been omitted from the trial balance.

   Calculate:

   (a) the balance of the suspense account after errors **i**, **ii** and **iii** were corrected

   (b) the balance of the petty cash book.

Review

There are more details about how to correct errors affecting the agreement of trial balance totals and how to prepare a suspense account in section 3.3 of *Essential Accounting for Cambridge IGCSE® & O Level (third edition)*, pages 118–20.

3.2.3 Correcting financial statements

Correcting an income statement

Errors in the books of account can lead to incorrect information being shown in the draft income statement. In these circumstances it is necessary to prepare a statement to amend the draft profit or loss.

Amendment	Type of error	Examples
Increase draft profit (or decrease draft loss)	When income has been omitted or understated, or where costs have been overstated	• Discounts received were omitted • Rent expenses were overstated because prepayment was overlooked
Decrease draft profit (or increase draft loss)	When income has been overstated, or where costs have been omitted or understated	• Returns inwards were not deducted from revenue • Depreciation was omitted
Double the amount involved	Where an entry has been made on the 'wrong side' of the income statement	• Discounts received were recorded as an expense
No effect	Errors in items which are not recorded in an income statement	• Trade payables were overstated

When preparing a statement to correct a draft profit figure, remember to give the statement a full title, to label each entry in the statement and to make it clear whether you are adding or subtracting the amount shown.

Correcting a statement of financial position

If there is a delay in correcting errors in the books of account, a draft financial statement could record incorrect information. Where the totals of the financial statement do not agree, a suspense account can be used to ensure agreement.

Correcting some errors can involve multiple changes to items on a statement of financial position. Here are some examples:

Error	Items affected	Corrections
No entry made for an irrecoverable debt	• trade receivables • profit for the year	• Reduce trade receivables • Reduce profit for the year
Inventory undervalued	• inventory • profit for the year	• Increase inventory • Increase profit for the year
Goods taken for own use not recorded	• drawings • profit for the year	• Increase drawings • Increase profit for the year*

*Inventory is not affected because the figure shown on the statement of financial position will be the amount actually in the stockroom at the year-end (and this will take account of the goods taken). Profit increases because the figure for purchases in the trading section of the income statement will have been overstated.

When correcting a draft statement of financial position, remember to set out detailed workings for any more complex calculations, particularly amendments to the draft profit figure.

Apply

5. A business has prepared an income statement, but there are uncorrected errors in the books of account. These errors include:

   i. overlooking the prepayment of insurance at the year end

   ii. the omission of depreciation of equipment from the income statement

   iii. overstating the balance of the drawings account

   iv. undervaluing the closing inventory

   v. omitting returns inwards from the income statement.

   For each error, state whether the draft profit would be increased, decreased, or unaffected when the error is corrected.

6. The totals of a business's statement of financial position did not agree, as total assets were greater than total capital and liabilities. The following errors were discovered:

   i. The balance of the cash account was overstated.

   ii. Carriage outwards was omitted from the income statement.

   iii. Depreciation of non-current assets was overstated.

   iv. No entries were made in the accounts for the settlement of the credit supplier account by cheque, minus a cash discount.

   State how each error would affect the statement of financial position in terms of:

   (a) non-current assets

   (b) current assets

   (c) capital

   (d) non-current liabilities

   (e) current liabilities.

Recap

1. Uncorrected errors in the books of account can lead to errors in preparing an income statement.

2. Any uncorrected error could increase the draft profit, decrease the draft profit, or have no effect.

3. If errors remain in the accounting system, the statement of financial position will also contain inaccuracies.

4. Errors can lead to multiple changes in the statement of financial position, including alterations to the profit or loss for the year.

Review

There is more information about correcting financial statements in section 3.4 of *Essential Accounting for Cambridge IGCSE® & O Level (third edition)*, pages 121–2.

You will need to know how to:

- explain the use and purpose of a bank statement
- update the cash book for bank charges, bank interest paid and received, correction of errors, credit transfers, direct debits, dividends and standing orders
- explain the purpose of, and prepare a bank reconciliation to include, bank errors, uncredited deposits and unpresented cheques.

Apply

1. A business's bank account balance was positive ($320) at the beginning of a month. During the month the following transactions affected the account:

    i. paid in $900 by cheque

    ii. paid in cash takings of $640

    iii. charged $80 for banking services.

    Calculate the balance to be shown on the business's bank statement after each transaction. In each case, identify whether the balance will be shown as debit or credit.

3.3.1 Bank statements

A **bank statement** is a copy of the bank's record of a customer's account, which is sent to the customer at regular intervals. Banks use the running balance layout, with three money columns (debit, credit, balance) and a new balance shown after each transaction.

The statement is prepared from the bank's point of view, so the balance shown on the account:

- is **credit**, where the customer has a positive balance – indicating the bank owes the customer this amount (i.e. a liability for the bank)
- is **debit**, where the customer has a negative (overdrawn) balance – indicating the bank is owed this amount by the customer (i.e. an asset for the bank).

Recap

1. A bank statement is a bank's record of the account of one of its customers.

2. If the customer's account has a positive balance it will appear as a credit balance on the bank statement (meaning the bank has a liability) but a debit balance in the customer's own records (i.e. an asset).

Review

There are examples of bank statements in sections 3.6 and 3.7 in *Essential Accounting for Cambridge IGCSE® & O Level (third edition)*, pages 130–3.

3.3.2 Updating cash books

When a bank statement is received, it is unlikely that the final balance shown will be the same as the balance on the cash book on that date. There are likely to be transactions recorded on the bank statement which have not yet been recorded in the cash book.

Transaction appearing on bank statement	Action to update cash book
Bank charge	Cr bank column
Bank interest paid (e.g. on an overdraft)	
Direct debit payment overlooked	
Standing order payment overlooked	
Dishonoured cheque (a cheque paid into the bank which has been not been accepted by the bank because the individual had insufficient funds in his or her account)	
Bank interest received directly by the bank (for example on an investment account)	Dr bank column
Dividend received directly by the bank	
Credit transfer (receipts from customers made directly to the bank)	

The cash book bank columns may also need to be amended if errors have been made in recording transactions.

Here is an example of the format for updating a cash book:

Dr				Cash book (bank columns)				Cr
2018			$	2018				$
Dec	31	Balance b/d	xxx	Dec	31	Bank charges		xxx
	31	Bank interest on savings account	xxx		31	Bank interest		xxx
	31	Dividends on investment	xxx		31	Electricity (DD)		xxx
	31	Trade receivable (credit transfer)	xxx		31	Rent (SO)		xxx
					31	Trade receivable (dishonoured cheque)		xxx
					31	Balance c/d		xxx
			xxx					xxx
2019								
Jan	1	Balance b/d	xxx					

✎ Apply

2. At the end of the month a business's cash book showed $1,980 in debit. However, the bank statement at this date included several items not yet recorded in the cash book:

   i.   a direct debit payment of $920

   ii. a credit transfer from a credit customer ($420)

   iii. bank charges of $80.

   Calculate an updated cash book balance after each of the items is included in the cash book.

3. A cash book's closing balance was $480 (credit). The cash book needs to be updated for some items shown on the bank statement:

   i.   a standing order for $440

   ii. a dishonoured cheque from a trade receivable ($540)

   iii. interest received on an investment account ($410).

   It is also necessary to correct an error:

   iv. a payment by cheque to a credit supplier – $830 debited in error in the cash book.

   Calculate the updated cash book balance after each of the items has been included in the cash book.

◀◀ Recap

1. Cash book balances at a particular date rarely agree with the balance shown on the bank statement for the same date.

2. Cash books are updated for any transactions recorded on the bank statement which have been omitted from the cash book.

3. Sometimes it will also be necessary to correct errors in the cash book.

⏱ Review

There is more information about updating cash books in section 3.7 in *Essential Accounting for Cambridge IGCSE® & O Level (third edition)*, pages 132–3.

3.3.3 Bank reconciliation statements

The bank statement is also unlikely to be fully up to date. The reasons are as follows:

Transaction	Explanation
Uncredited deposits	Amounts paid into the bank and recorded in the cash book (e.g. from sales, or receipts from credit customers) which have not yet been recorded on the bank statement.
Unpresented cheques	Cheques which have been recorded in the cash book but have not yet been cleared by the bank and, therefore, have not yet been recorded on the bank statement.
Errors	Occasionally banks may make errors in recording transactions in customer accounts.

Where the bank statement is not up to date, a bank reconciliation is prepared to check whether the updated cash book and updated bank statement agree.

There are two formats for a bank reconciliation statement:

Option 1	
Bank reconciliation statement at (date)	
	$
Balance as per bank statement	xxx
Add: uncredited deposits	xxx
	xxx
Less: unpresented cheques	(xxx)
	xxx
Add/less error correction	xxx
Balance as per cash book	xxx

Option 2	
Bank reconciliation statement at (date)	
	$
Balance as per cash book	xxx
Less: uncredited deposits	(xxx)
	xxx
Add: unpresented cheques	xxx
	xxx
Add/less error correction	xxx
Balance as per bank statement	xxx

Particular care is required if the bank balance is overdrawn, as any amendments in the statement will be added or subtracted as appropriate to a negative figure.

Where the updated balances agree, it can be assumed that the cash book record is error free.

Recap

1. Bank statements will rarely be up to date and will not show some transactions currently recorded in a cash book.

2. A bank reconciliation is prepared to show how the balance shown by the bank statement would change if it were up to date.

Review

There is an illustration of the bank reconciliation process in section 3.8 of *Essential Accounting for Cambridge IGCSE® & O Level (third edition)*, pages 134–6.

Apply

4. At the end of the month a business's bank statement recorded a credit balance of $1,840. However, the bank statement omitted:

   i. some cash takings (uncredited deposits of $1,590) paid into the bank account towards the end of the month

   ii. unpresented cheques totalling $2,390.

   What was the balance shown in the business's updated cash book at this date?

5. A business's bank statement recorded an overdrawn balance of $840 at the end of the month. The bank statement omitted:

   i. unpresented cheques of $630

   ii. uncredited deposits of $2,030.

   What was the balance of the business's updated cash book at this date?

You will need to know how to:

- explain the purposes of purchases ledger and sales ledger control accounts
- identify the books of prime entry as sources of information for control account entries
- prepare purchases ledger and sales ledger control accounts.

3.4.1 The role and use of control accounts

Control accounts are used to check the accuracy of the personal accounts of credit suppliers in the purchases ledger, and credit customers in the sales ledger.

Control accounts help to locate errors where the totals of a trial balance have failed to agree. They are memorandum accounts – meaning they are not part of the double-entry system.

They have some additional benefits:

- They provide immediate information about total trade payables and total trade receivables when preparing a statement of financial position.

- They act as an independent check on the work of the accounts personnel preparing the purchases and sales ledger, and so can help reduce the chance of fraud.

Sources of information for control accounts

Any transaction which affects a purchases ledger account will need to be included in the **purchases ledger control account**. Totals for each of these items are required for entry in the control account.

Purchases ledger control account	
Main items	**Source of information**
Opening balance of amounts owing to trade payables	Balance b/d from previous control account
Credit purchases	Purchases book
Payments to trade payables	Cash book
Discounts received	Cash book
Purchases returns	Purchases returns book
Other items	
Refunds by credit suppliers	Cash book
Interest charged by suppliers on overdue accounts	Journal
Contra entries	Journal

Any transaction which affects a sales ledger account will need to be included in the **sales ledger control account**. Totals for each of these items are required for entry in the control account.

Sales ledger control account	
Main items	**Source of information**
Opening balance of amounts owed by trade receivables	Balance b/d from previous control account
Credit sales	Sales book
Receipts from trade receivables	Cash book
Discounts allowed	Cash book
Sales returns	Purchases returns book
Other items	
Refunds to credit customers	Cash book
Interest charged to customers on overdue accounts	Journal
Irrecoverable debts	Journal
Dishonoured cheques	Cash book
Contra entries	Journal

Contra entries in control accounts occur in the following circumstances.

- The business is both a supplier and a customer of another organization.

- Separate accounts are maintained for acting as a supplier and for acting as a customer.

- By agreement, the balance of one account is 'set off' against the balance of the other account to find the net balance.

- The net balance could be due to the other organization or owed by the other organization.

- The contra entry is recorded first in the journal and then in each of the personal accounts.

Balance on both sides of control accounts

The account of a trade payable could occasionally have a debit balance. This is usually because the supplier has been overpaid. Any debit balances on the accounts of trade payables are shown separately in the purchases ledger control account, both as opening balances and as closing balances.

Similarly, the accounts of a trade receivable could have a credit balance if the customer has overpaid. Any credit balances on the accounts of trade receivables are shown separately in the sales ledger control account, both as opening balances and as closing balances.

Recap

1. Control accounts are a check on the accuracy of the sales ledger and the purchases ledger.

2. Control accounts also provide information for use in financial statements and can help deter fraud.

3. Control accounts record total entries for transactions which have affected credit suppliers (purchases ledger control account) and credit customers (sales ledger control account).

4. Totals are taken from books of prime entry.

5. Control accounts also include opening balances brought down from the previous period's control accounts.

6. Control accounts conclude with closing balances, which should agree with the total of balances in the purchases ledger and sales ledger.

7. Occasionally, a sales ledger account can have a credit balance, and this must be reflected in the sales control account for that period.

8. Occasionally, a purchases ledger account can have a debit balance, and this must be reflected in the purchases ledger control account for that period.

Apply

1. A purchases ledger control account is being prepared. State the source for each of the following entries:

    (a) opening balance of the control account

    (b) credit purchases

    (c) payments to credit suppliers

    (d) interest charged by suppliers on overdue accounts

    (e) contra entries with the sales ledger.

2. A sales ledger control account is being prepared. State the source for each of the following entries:

    (a) discounts allowed

    (b) returns inwards

    (c) irrecoverable debts

    (d) dishonoured cheques

    (e) total of closing credit balances.

Review

There is more information about purchases ledger control accounts and sales ledger control accounts in sections 3.9–3.12 in *Essential Accounting for Cambridge IGCSE® & O Level (third edition)*, pages 145–151.

3.4.2 Control account formats

Purchases ledger control account for (month, year)

	$		$
Opening balance b/d (the total of any credit suppliers' accounts who have overpaid)	xxx	Opening balance b/d (the total of amounts owed to credit suppliers)	xxx
Bank (payments to credit suppliers)	xxx	Credit purchases	xxx
Discounts received	xxx	Interest charged on overdue accounts	xxx
Contras with sales ledger	xxx	Refunds	xxx
Purchases returns	xxx	Closing balance c/d (the total of any credit suppliers' accounts who have overpaid)	xxx
Closing c/d (the total of amounts owed to credit suppliers)	xxx		
	xxx		xxx
Balance b/d	xxx	Balance b/d	xxx

Sales ledger control account for (month, year)

	$		$
Opening balance b/d (the total of amounts owed by credit customers)	xxx	Opening balance b/d (the total of any customers' accounts who have overpaid)	xxx
Credit sales	xxx	Bank (receipts from credit customers)	xxx
Dishonoured cheques	xxx	Discounts allowed	xxx
Refunds	xxx	Sales returns	xxx
Interest on overdue accounts	xxx	Irrecoverable debts	xxx
Closing balance c/d (the total of any credit customers' accounts who have overpaid)	xxx	Contras with purchases ledger	xxx
		Closing balance c/d (the total of amounts owed by credit customers)	xxx
	xxx		xxx
Balance b/d	xxx	Balance b/d	xxx

⊗ Common errors

- Don't forget that a contra entry between personal ledger accounts affects both the purchases ledger control account and the sales ledger control account.
- Don't forget to bring down the closing balance on a control account.

Recap

1. A purchases ledger control account closely resembles a purchases ledger account. Increases in the amount due to credit suppliers are credited to the account, and decreases are debited to the account.

2. A sales ledger control account closely resembles a sales ledger account. Increases in the amount due from credit customers are debited to the account and decreases are credited to the account.

Apply

3. A purchases ledger control account is being prepared. State on which side of the account each of the following should be recorded:

   i.   discounts received

   ii. credit purchases

   iii. interest charged by suppliers on overdue accounts

   iv. closing balance of amounts due to credit suppliers to carry down.

4. A sales ledger control account is being prepared. State on which side of the account each of the following should be recorded:

   i.   returns inwards

   ii. receipts from credit customers

   iii. interest charged on overdue accounts of credit customers

   iv. refunds to credit customers who have overpaid

   v.   contra entries with the purchases ledger.

Review

There are full illustrations of purchases ledger control accounts and sales ledger control accounts in sections 3.10 and 3.12 in *Essential Accounting for Cambridge IGCSE® & O Level (third edition)*, pages 146–7 and 150–1.

Exam-style questions

1. Mandeep, a trainee accountant, has prepared the following trial balance on 31 December 2018. It contains some errors.

Trial balance	Dr	Cr
	$	$
Administration expenses	1 850	
Bank (overdrawn)	2 480	
Capital		90 000
Carriage outwards		820
Cash in hand	1 090	
Discounts allowed		320
Discounts received	170	
Drawings	13 580	
General expenses	3 650	
Inventory:		
at 1 January 2018	11 460	
at 31 December 2018	10 230	
Loan from GK Finance	8 000	
Non-current assets		65 000
Purchases	72 890	
Returns inwards		360
Returns outwards	1 010	
Revenue		103 400
Trade payables	16 730	
Trade receivables		8 440
Wages	32 330	
	175 470	268 340

Mandeep has made an error of commission: he has recorded an administration expense of $350 as a general expense.

Mandeep has also made an error of complete reversal. The payment of wages in cash $470 has been debited to the cash account and credited to the wages account.

Prepare a corrected trial balance. **(16)**

Before you answer the question

It is suggested you work through the existing trial balance and mark off any items which are recorded in the wrong column.

It could also be helpful to change any figures which are incorrect as a result of the errors made by Mandeep.

Check your answer

To help you identify changes, alterations to the original trial balance are shown in bold.

Trial balance at 31 December 2018			
	Dr	Cr	
	$	$	
Administration expenses	**2200**		**(1)**
Bank (overdrawn)		**2480**	**(1)**
Capital		90000	
Carriage outwards	**820**		**(1)**
Cash in hand	**150**		**(2)**
Discounts allowed	**320**		**(1)**
Discounts received		**170**	**(1)**
Drawings	13580		
General expenses	**3300**		**(1)**
Inventory:			
at 1 January 2018	11460		
at 31 December 2018			
Loan from GK Finance		8000	
Non-current assets	**65000**		**(1)**
Purchases	72890		
Returns inwards	**360**		**(1)**
Returns outwards		**1010**	**(1)**
Revenue		103400	
Trade payables		**16730**	**(1)**
Trade receivables	**8440**		**(1)**
Wages	**33270**		**(2)**
	211790	**221790**	**(1)**

Common errors

Remember to:

- give the trial balance a full title, including the date

- double the amount when correcting the error of reversal (here this affects the cash and wages figures)

- look for items which were recorded in the wrong column in the original trial balance.

Exam tip

If there are mistakes in your answer, write a correction together with a brief note to remind yourself of what went wrong.

For example, if you did not give the trial balance a proper title, change your answer to include the date and write a note alongside this saying something like 'trial balances should have a full date in the title'.

Each correction you make to your answer will improve your performance.

2. Darim prepared a trial balance on 31 December 2018 but the totals did not agree. The debit column totalled $163 130 and the credit column totalled $157 280. Darim has checked the accounts and has discovered all the errors which caused the difference:

   i. The total of the sales book for December, $3,820, was not posted to the nominal ledger.

   ii. An invoice from a supplier, KX Ltd, for $3,470, was entered in the purchases book as $3,740.

   iii. A receipt of $720 from a credit customer, T Williams, was credited to the account of J Williamson.

   iv. Cash sales of $1,480 were correctly entered in the sales account, but were recorded as $1,840 in the cash book.

   v. The balance of the returns inwards account was overstated by $190.

   vi. The total of the returns outwards book for December, $740, was posted to the debit side of the returns outwards book.

   (a) Prepare journal entries to correct the errors. **(18)**

   (b) Prepare the suspense account. **(5)**

   (c) Complete the following table to show the effect of correcting each error on the business's draft profit for the year ended 31 December 2018. Place a tick in the relevant column to indicate whether the draft profit would be increased, decreased, or would not be affected by correcting the error. The first error has been answered as an example.

Common errors

Remember to:

- recognize when a correction involves the suspense account and when it does not

- use the correct format for a journal entry, including a narrative (when required by the question)

- transfer entries to the suspense account correctly based on the entries in the general journal

- close the suspense account.

	Effect on profit when the error is corrected		
Error	Increase	Decrease	Not affected
i.	✔		
ii.			
iii.			
iv.			
v.			
vi.			

(5)

(Total marks: 28)

Before you answer the question

Remember that a journal entry should start with the account to be debited and be followed by the account to be credited.

A narrative is required for each journal entry and this should fully explain the reasons for the entry.

The six errors contain a mix of those which affect the suspense account and those which do not. It is suggested that each error is checked for which category it falls into before preparing the journal entries.

If you find it difficult to decide on the correct entries to make for any of the errors, a useful tip is to roughly draw up the accounts affected. This may help you visualize the way to correct the error.

Check your answer

2. (a)

			GENERAL JOURNAL	Dr	Cr	
Error	2018			$	$	
1	Dec	31	Suspense	3 820		**(1)**
			Sales		3 820	**(1)**
			Correction of error: sales book total was not posted to the nominal ledger			**(1)**
2		31	Account payable: KX Ltd	270		**(1)**
			Purchases		270	**(1)**
			Correction of error of original entry: amount of invoice from supplier misread			**(1)**
3		31	Account receivable: J Williamson	720		**(1)**
			Account receivable: T Williams		720	**(1)**
			Correction of error of commission: receipt recorded in the wrong sales ledger account			**(1)**
4		31	Suspense	360		**(1)**
			Cash		360	**(1)**
			Correction of incorrect recording of value of cash sales in the cash account			**(1)**
5		31	Suspense	190		**(1)**
			Returns inwards		190	**(1)**
			Correction of error: overstated balance of account			**(1)**
6		31	Suspense	1 480		**(1)**
			Returns outwards		1 480	**(1)**
			Correction of entry on wrong side of account			**(1)**

(b)

Dr			Suspense account					Cr	
2018				$		2018			$
Dec	31	Sales		3 820	**(1)**	Dec	31	Difference in trial balance	5 850	**(1)**
	31	Cash		360	**(1)**				
	31	Returns inwards		190	**(1)**				
	31	Returns outwards		1 480	**(1)**				
				5 850					5 850

(c)

	Effect on profit when the error is corrected			
Error	Increase	Decrease	Not be affected	
1	✔			
2	✔			**(1)**
3			✔	**(1)**
4			✔	**(1)**
5	✔			**(1)**
6	✔			**(1)**

3. Wei has been comparing his bank statement and cash book for the month of November 2018:

ANYBANK plc					
Bank Statement for Wei's Retail Store					
Date	Details	Dr	Cr	Balance	
2018		$	$	$	
Nov 1	Balance			930	Cr
4	39422	290		640	Cr
8	DD Regional Electrics	670		30	Dr
12	39423	1 320		1 350	Dr
15	Sundries		2 130	780	Cr
20	SO City Properties plc	1 420		640	Dr
24	Credit transfer – Samah Stores		950	310	Cr
28	M Lall (dishonoured cheque)	830		520	Dr
29	CHR	110		630	Dr

BOOKS OF WEI'S RETAIL STORE					
CASH BOOK (Bank columns only)					
Dr					Cr
2018			**2018**		
Nov 1	Balance	930	Nov 2	General expenses (chq 39422)	290
13	Sales	2 130	9	Carson Wholesale (chq 39423)	1 320
28	Sales	2 890	23	PQZ Ltd (chq 39424)	740
			24	Rent (Standing order)	1 420
			28	Drawings (chq 39425)	480
			30	Balance c/d	1 700
		5 950			5 950
Dec 1	Balance b/d	1 700			

(a) List the items in the bank statement which have not yet been recorded in the cash book. **(4)**

(b) List the items in the cash book which have not yet been recorded in the bank statement. **(3)**

(c) Prepare an updated cash book and balance on 30 November 2018. **(6)**

(d) Prepare a bank reconciliation statement at 30 November 2018. **(4)**

(Total marks: 17)

Before you answer the question

Take time to compare the two documents. The recommended procedure is to tick items which appear in both the bank statement and the cash book (including the opening balance).

List the items as required by tasks **(a)** and **(b)**. This will help with tasks **(c)** and **(d)**.

Remember: if you are deducting a figure from an overdraft, the overdraft increases in value, and vice versa.

Check your answer

3. **(a)**
   - 8 Nov: DD Regional Electrics $670 **(1)**
   - 24 Nov: Credit transfer Samah Stores $950 **(1)**
   - 28 Nov: M Lall dishonoured cheque $830 **(1)**
   - 29 Nov: Charges $110 **(1)**

   (b)
   - 23 Nov: Cheque 39424 PZQ Ltd $740 **(1)**
   - 28 Nov: Cash sales $2,890 **(1)**
   - 28 Nov: Cheque 39425 Drawings $480 **(1)**

> **Exam tip**
>
> As always, make a point of spending a little time correcting your mistakes and working on understanding why the model answer was different from your own. This will be time well spent!

(c)

CASH BOOK (Bank columns only)							
Dr							**Cr**
2018			$		2018		$
Dec	1	Balance b/d	1700 **(1)**		Dec 1	Electricity (DD Regional Electrics)	670 **(1)**
	1	Samah Stores (credit transfer)	950 **(1)**		1	M Lall (dishonoured cheque)	830 **(1)**
					1	Bank charges	110 **(1)**
					1	Balance c/d	1040
			2650				2650
Dec	1	Balance b/d	1040 **(1of)**				

(d)

Option 1		
Bank reconciliation statement at 1 December 2018		
	$	$
Balance as per bank statement (overdrawn)		(630) **(1)**
Add: uncredited deposits		2890 **(1)**
		2260
Less: unpresented cheques		
39424 PQZ Ltd	740	
39425 Drawings	480	
		1220 **(1)**
Balance as per cash book		1040 **(1)**

Option 2		
Bank reconciliation statement at 1 December 2018		
	$	$
Balance as per cash book		1040 **(1)**
Less: uncredited deposits		(2890) **(1)**
		(1850)
Add: unpresented cheques		
39424 PQZ Ltd	740	
39425 Drawings	480	
		1220 **(1)**
Balance as per bank statement (overdrawn)		(630) **(1)**

Exam tip

Make a point of altering any mistakes in your answer and adding a note about what you did wrong. Each alteration you make will mark another step forward in improving your performance.

4. A bookkeeper prepared control accounts from the following information:

	$
Total balances at 1 September 2018	
Purchases ledger – credit balances	14 300
Sales ledger – debit balances	17 290
Sales ledger – credit balances	330
Totals from books of prime entry	
Purchases journal	156 700
Sales journal	248 350
Purchases returns journal	3 410
Sales returns journal	2 990
Cash book	
Payments to credit suppliers	152 230
Receipts from credit customers	241 370
Cash sales	38 430
Cash purchases	9 520
Discounts allowed	2 240
Discounts received	1 940
Dishonoured cheques	830
Refunds from credit suppliers	450
General journal	
Irrecoverable debts	1 080
Contras: purchases ledger accounts set off against sales ledger accounts	3 470
Interest charged by suppliers on overdue accounts	410
Increase in provision for doubtful debts	360
Total of debit balances in purchases ledger at 30 September 2018	320

(a) Prepare a purchases ledger control account for September 2018. **(10)**

(b) Prepare a sales ledger control account for September 2018. **(10)**

(Total marks: 20)

Before you answer the question

It is suggested you work your way through the list of items marking out those for the purchases ledger control account, those for the sales ledger control account and those which should be ignored as they do not affect the personal accounts of credit suppliers and credit customers.

Check your answer

4. (a)

Purchases ledger control account for September 2018					
	$			$	
Bank	152 230	**(1)**	Opening balance b/d	14 300	**(1)**
Discounts received	1 940	**(1)**	Credit purchases	156 700	**(1)**
Purchases returns	3 410	**(1)**	Interest charged on overdue accounts	410	**(1)**
Contras with sales ledger	3 470	**(1)**	Refunds	450	**(1)**
Closing c/d	11 120		Closing balance c/d	310	
	172 170			172 170	
Balance b/d	310	**(1)**	Balance b/d	11 120	**(1)**

(b)

Sales ledger control account for September 2018					
	$			$	
Opening balance b/d	17 290	(1)	Opening balance b/d	330	(1)
Credit sales	248 350	(1)	Bank	241 370	(1)
Dishonoured cheques	830	(1)	Discounts allowed	2 240	(1)
			Sales returns	2 990	(1)
			Irrecoverable debts	1 080	(1)
			Contras with purchases ledger	3 470	(1)
			Closing balance c/d	14 990	
	266 470			266 470	
Balance b/d	14 990	(1)			

Multiple choice questions

1. Which of the following account balances appears in the credit column of a trial balance? **(1)**

A   carriage outwards
B   discounts allowed
C   purchases
D   returns outwards

2. Which of the following account balances appears in the debit column of a trial balance? **(1)**

A   bank loan
B   discounts received
C   returns inwards
D   trade payables

3. A bookkeeper overlooked an invoice for goods, $700, when preparing a business's accounting records.

Which type of error did the bookkeeper make? **(1)**

A   error of commission
B   error of omission
C   error of original entry
D   error of principle

4. Which of the following errors affects agreement of a trial balance totals? **(1)**

A   credit note from a trade payable $110 entered in the returns journal as $100

B   machine repairs debited to the machinery account

C   payment of rent entered correctly in bank account and credited to the rent account

D   receipt from debtor debited to bank but credited to trade payable account.

5. An account balance of $50 has been entered on the credit side of a trial balance instead of the debit side. How will the trial balance totals be affected? **(1)**

A   The credit side will be greater than the debit side by $50.
B   The credit side will be greater than the debit side by $100.
C   The debit side will be greater than the credit side by $50.
D   The debit side will be greater than the credit side by $100.

6. Shakira's trial balance totals did not agree. The debit column total was $17 220 and credit column total was $17 380. Shakira found the following errors:

- The total of the returns inwards book ($160) had not been posted to the nominal ledger.

Common errors

Remember to:

- give a proper title to each of the control accounts
- include all necessary items
- omit cash purchases, cash sales and increases in provisions for doubtful debts
- check items have been entered on the right sides of control accounts
- include the contra entry in both control accounts
- bring down the balances on the control accounts.

Exam tip

If you have made errors, make alternations to your answer. Check you understand why you went wrong and indicate how the right answer is obtained, by writing in the alternations. This process will always improve your performance.

- No entry had been made for the value of goods taken for own use by the owner, $80.

The errors were corrected and the trial balance totals agreed. What were the totals of the corrected trial balance? **(1)**

A $17140   **B** $17300   **C** $17380   **D** $17460

7. Yasmin has compared her cash book with her bank statement. Which of the following items will decrease the balance in her cash book? **(1)**

A credit transfer from a credit customer

B dishonoured cheque from a credit customer

C uncredited deposits

D unpresented cheques

8. Abdul has compared his cash book and bank statement and he has updated his cash book. Which of the following items will appear in the bank reconciliation statement? **(1)**

A bank charges

B credit transfer from a credit customer

C correction of error in bank columns of cash book

D uncredited deposits

9. Maria received her bank statement on 31 March 2019. On this date the statement recorded a balance of $100 marked 'Cr'. On this date there were unpresented cheques of $600 and an uncredited deposit of $800. What balance should appear in Maria's updated cash book on 31 March 2019? **(1)**

A credit $100   **C** debit $100

B credit $300   **D** debit $300

10. Which sources of information are used when preparing control accounts? **(1)**

A books of prime entry   **C** ledger accounts

B invoices   **D** trial balances

11. Which one of the following should be entered on the debit side of a purchases ledger control account? **(1)**

A contras with sales ledger accounts

B credit purchases

C discounts allowed

D refunds from credit suppliers

12. A sales ledger control account contained the following items:

	$
Debit balance at beginning of the period	9 500
Credit sales	11 800
Interest charges on overdue accounts	400
Receipts from accounts receivables	10 800

What was the closing balance of the sales ledger control account? **(1)**

A $8100   **C** $10100

B $8900   **D** $10900

(Total marks: 12)

Structured questions

1. Describe **(a)** one benefit and **(b)** one limitation of preparing trial balances. **(2)**

2. Thembi has provided the following list of balances from her business's accounting system at 31 March 2018.

	$
Bank loan	11 500
Bank loan interest	840
Capital	80 480
Cash at bank	3 720
Carriage inwards	810
Carriage outwards	630
Discounts received	590
Drawings	18 450
Insurance	3 720
Inventory at 1 April 2017	11 910
Motor vehicles	35 680
Petty cash in hand	50
Premises	72 000
Purchases	84 270
Repairs and maintenance costs	1 360
Returns inwards	480
Returns outwards	660
Revenue	163 500
Salaries	27 200
Trade payables	11 820
Trade receivables	7 430

She has been checking these accounts and she has noticed two errors:

- a payment for motor vehicle maintenance for $370 has been debited to the motor vehicles account

- an invoice received from a credit supplier for $560 has been entered in the accounts as $650.

(a) Prepare a trial balance at 31 March 2018 having corrected the two errors. **(2)**

(b) Identify the type of error made for the value of motor vehicle maintenance charges. **(1)**

(c) Identify the type of error made when the invoice was incorrectly recorded. **(1)**

3. **(a)** Describe what is meant by an error of commission. **(2)**

(b) When Abdul prepared a trial balance for his business the totals did not agree and the difference was entered in a suspense account. The trial balance totals were Dr $115 140 and Cr $115 450.

Explain on which side of a suspense account the opening balance should be recorded. **(2)**

Abdul discovered the following errors which accounted for the difference in the trial balance totals:

- the total of the discounts received column in the cash book, $130, had not been posted to the nominal ledger

- a cheque in payment of general expenses ($120) had been recorded in the accounts as $210

- Abdul had withdrawn goods for his own use, to the value of $240. The only entry made for this transaction was to debit the drawings account with $240

- the balance of the carriage outwards account had been undercast by $140

- the only entry made for the receipt of a cheque from a credit customer was to credit the bank account with $540.

(c) Prepare journal entries to correct these errors (narratives are not required). **(11)**

(d) Prepare a suspense account. **(5)**

4. Lydia has discovered that some errors were made when preparing her business's accounting records for the year ended 31 December 2018:

- in a purchases invoice for goods for resale, $11600, had been incorrectly entered in the books as $10600

- carriage outwards of $530 had been treated as carriage inwards

- no account had been taken of rent received in advance of $450

- discounts received of $80 had not been posted to the sales ledger

- the closing inventory had been overvalued by $270.

The draft profit for the year ended on that date was $45320.

Prepare a statement to show a corrected profit for the year ended 31 December 2018. **(7)**

5. An inexperienced bookkeeper prepared the following statement of financial position at 30 June 2018.

Statement of financial position for the year ending 30 June 2018			
	$	$	$
Non-current assets			83500
Current assets			
Inventory	14900		
Trade receivables	11530		
Bank overdraft	3200		
		29630	
Less Current liabilities			
Bank loan (repayable 2022)	5000		
Trade payables	9450		
		14450	
			15180
			98680
Capital			
Opening balance		80080	
Add profit for the year		34630	
		114710	
Less drawings		22430	
			92280

The following errors were discovered:

- inventory had been undervalued by $1,420

- a payment to a credit supplier by cheque $850 had been overlooked

- the owner had withdrawn goods for her own use, $310, but no entries had been made for this transaction

- a payment by cheque $1,100 for some additional non-current assets had been entered twice in the books.

Prepare a corrected statement of financial position at 30 June 2018.   **(10)**

6. Kadema has compared her cash book and bank statement. On 31 October 2018 both documents recorded a positive balance: the cash book balance was debit $870, but the balance on the bank statement was $210 Cr.

    (a) Explain why the cash book balance is shown on the debit side, why the bank statement balance is marked 'Cr'.   **(2)**

    The following discrepancies between the two records were found:

    - a standing order payment for rent $840 had not been recorded in the cash book

    - bank charges of $80 had been omitted from the cash book

    - there was an uncredited deposit of $930

    - the bank statement included a credit transfer of $390 from TQ Ltd which had not been recorded in the cash book

    - there was an unpresented cheque for $610

    - the bank statement recorded a dishonoured cheque for $340 from HZ Ltd, but this had been shown as $430 in the cash book.

    (b) Prepare an updated cash book to show an amended balance on 31 October 2018.   **(6)**

    (c) Prepare a bank reconciliation statement dated 31 October 2018.   **(4)**

7. Asif is a bookkeeper employed by Palmford Retail Stores. On 31 August 2018 the business's bank balance recorded in the cash book was overdrawn $2,360. This did not agree with the balance shown on the bank statement at this date.

    Asif has compared the two documents and has discovered the following differences:

    - a direct debit for insurance $170 has been omitted from the cash book

    - cash takings of $1,230 were deposited with the bank early in August 2018. This has been correctly recorded in the cash book, but it is shown as $1,030 on the bank statement

    - a cheque received from a credit customer, M Jones, for $1,210 has been recorded in the cash book but it is shown on the bank statement as being dishonoured

    - a dividend of $410 on some investments appears in the bank statement but not in the cash book

- there are unpresented cheques: TLX Ltd $390 and Ramanjeet Retail $720

- there are uncredited deposits totalling $1,430.

(a) Compare a direct debit and a standing order. Describe the differences between these methods of payment. **(4)**

(b) Prepare an updated cash book to shown an amended balance on 31 August 2018. **(5)**

(c) Prepare a bank reconciliation statement dated 31 August 2018. **(5)**

8. Sophia is responsible for preparing the sales ledger control account for JK Stores Ltd in order to check the accuracy of the sales ledger.

(a) Describe **two** benefits of preparing a sales ledger control account other than checking the accuracy of the sales ledger. **(4)**

She has selecting the following information for the month of November 2018:

	$
Debit balance of control account on 1 November 2018	18 420
Totals from books of prime entry	
Sales book	28 480
Sales returns book	1 450
Cash book	
Receipts from credit customers	27 440
Discounts allowed	610
Refunds to credit customers	390
Dishonoured cheques	630
General journal	
Irrecoverable debts written off	610
Contra entries with purchases ledger accounts	520
Total of credit balances in sales ledger at 30 November 2018	270

(b) Prepare the sales ledger control account for November 2018. **(11)**

The total debit balances in the sales ledger at 30 November 2018 was $17 120.

(c) Explain what conclusions you would draw from this information. **(2)**

9. An inexperienced bookkeeper was preparing a business's purchases ledger control account for September 2018.

(a) Explain how preparing control accounts can reduce the chances of fraud. **(2)**

(b) The bookkeeper has selected the following information:

	$
Purchases ledger control accounts balances at 1 September 2018	
Debit	3 980
Credit	24 760
Cash purchases	5 330
Credit purchases	22 970
Payments to credit suppliers	24 240
Discounts allowed	1 430
Discounts received	990
Purchases returns	550
Contra entries between the sales and purchases ledgers	410
Refunds from credit suppliers	200
Interest charged on overdue accounts by credit suppliers	150
Total of accounts payable with debit balances at 30 September 2018	2 440

Prepare the purchases ledger control account for September 2018. **(11)**

The total of credit balances in the purchases ledger at 30 September 2018 was $20 350.

(c) Explain what conclusions you would draw from this information. **(3)**

(Total marks: 102)

Unit 4:
Accounting procedures

Unit outline

It is important that those who use accounting records and financial statements can have confidence in the information with which they are presented. Central to this is knowing that profits or losses properly reflect a business's performance over a financial period.

This unit provides details of the techniques which are used to ensure profits are measured so as to give a true and fair picture of a business's performance.

Either tick these boxes to build a record of your revision, or use them to identify your strengths and weaknesses.

Your revision checklist

Specification	Theme	☺	☺	☹
4.1 Capital and revenue	4.1.1 Capital expenditure and revenue expenditure			
	4.1.2 Capital expenditure and revenue receipts			
	4.1.3 The effect of incorrect treatment of revenue and capital items on profit and asset valuations			
4.2 Depreciation	4.2.1 Depreciation: background			
	4.2.2 Ledger and journal entries to record depreciation			
	4.2.3 The disposal of a non-current asset			
4.3 Adjustments	4.3.1 Expense adjustments			
	4.3.2 Income adjustments			
4.4 Irrecoverable debts and provision for doubtful debts	4.4.1 Irrecoverable debts and recovery of debts written off			
	4.4.2 Recording irrecoverable debts			
	4.4.3 Recording recovery of debts written off			
	4.4.4 Provision for doubtful debts			
	4.4.5 Recording provision for doubtful debts			
4.5 Valuation of inventory	4.5.1 The rule for the valuation of inventory			
	4.5.2 The effects of an incorrect valuation of inventory			

You will need to know how to:

- distinguish between and account for capital expenditure and revenue expenditure
- distinguish between and account for capital receipts and revenue receipts
- calculate and comment on the effect of incorrect treatment on profit and asset valuations.

4.1.1 Capital expenditure and revenue expenditure

Capital expenditure is money spent on non-current assets.

What the term includes	Examples
Purchasing a non-current asset	Purchase of land, premises, machinery, equipment, motor vehicles, furniture, fittings, etc.
Improving a non-current asset	Building an extension to premises Installing air conditioning in premises
Getting a non-current asset ready for use	Carriage costs paid when purchasing machinery Wages paid to employees for installing a new machine Legal costs paid when purchasing premises

Capital expenditure does not include repairs and maintenance costs, because it is assumed these costs do not improve the non-current asset or increase its value.

Capital expenditure is recorded on a statement of financial position. Depreciation charges are based on the total capital expenditure on a non-current asset. Capital expenditure is assumed to benefit a business for a long period (more than one financial year).

Revenue expenditure is money spent on the day-to-day expenses of running a business.

What the term includes	Examples
Administration expenses	Postage, stationery and telephone expenses Office manager's salary Wages of accounts department staff Maintenance of office equipment
Selling and distribution expenses	Carriage inwards Carriage outwards Selling expenses Repairs to delivery vehicle Wages of sales staff
Finance costs	Loan interest Debenture interest (limited company)

Revenue expenditure is charged to the income statement. It is assumed to benefit the business for a short period (less than one financial year).

 Recap

1. Capital expenditure is money spent on purchasing and improving non-current assets; it is recorded in the statement of financial position.

2. Revenue expenditure is money spent on the day-to-day running costs of a business; it is recorded in the income statement.

3. Certain expenses (such as wages paid to install new machinery) are regarded as capital expenditure because they benefit the business for a long time.

4. Certain expense payments relating to non-current assets are regarded as revenue expenditure (such as repairs) because they do not add to the value of the non-current asset.

Review

There are more details about capital and revenue expenditure in section 4.4 of *Essential Accounting for Cambridge IGCSE® & O Level (third edition)*, pages 165–6.

Recap

1. Capital receipts arise from one-off non-trading activities, such as additional investment by the owner(s) in the business, loans and the sale of non-current assets. Capital receipts are not recorded in the income statement

2. Revenue receipts arise from routine business activities such as sales of goods and services and other income. Revenue receipts are recorded in the income statement.

Apply

3. During a recent month Duchan's cash book recorded the following receipts: fees from clients $3,200; loan from a finance company $4,000; sale of unwanted furniture $300; interest received on an investment $100; rent received from a tenant $500.

   (a) Calculate the total amount of capital receipts.

   (b) Calculate the total amount of revenue receipts.

Apply

1. Jody has just purchased a second-hand delivery vehicle for business use. She has paid $15 000 for the motor vehicle, $3,000 to ensure it was in full working order, $1,500 for adding new shelving to the interior of the vehicle, $400 for insuring the vehicle for the next six months and $600 for adding the business logo to the side of the vehicle. State which of the items should be regarded as:

   i. capital expenditure   ii. revenue expenditure.

2. Rakesh has purchased new machinery for his business. The machinery cost $36 000. He paid $1,500 for the machinery to be delivered to his business premises and $2,500 wages to his staff for installing the machine. Rakesh intends to depreciate the machinery by 20 per cent per annum using the straight-line method. Calculate the annual depreciation charge on the machinery.

4.1.2 Capital expenditure and revenue receipts

Capital receipts are amounts received from one-off non-trading activities.

What the term includes	Examples
Additional capital	Additional investment in a business by the owner(s) (sole traders and partnerships)
	Issue of shares (limited companies)
Borrowing	Bank loans
	Mortgages
	Debentures (limited companies)
Sales of non-current assets	Sale of unwanted machinery
	Sale of equipment at the end of its useful life

Capital receipts are not included in the income statement. In the case of the sale of non-current assets, only any loss or profit made on a disposal is recorded in the income statement.

Revenue receipts are amounts received from normal business activities.

What the term includes	Examples
Revenue	Sale of goods (trading business)
	Fees from clients (service businesses)
Other income	Rent received
	Commission received
	Interest received

Revenue receipts are recorded in the income statement. In a trading business, revenue is recorded in the trading section and other income is recorded in the profit and loss section.

Review

There are more details about capital and revenue receipts in section 4.5 of *Essential Accounting for Cambridge IGCSE® & O Level (third edition)*, pages 167–8.

4.1.3 The effect of incorrect treatment of revenue and capital items on profit and asset valuations

When mistakes are made recording revenue and capital items in the financial statements it will mean that:

- profits and losses will be incorrect

- asset valuations on the statement of financial position will be incorrect

- the analysis of a business's performance will be affected because ratio calculations will show the wrong results

- decisions made by owners, managers and other interested parties are likely to be misguided because they are based on incorrect information.

Results of incorrect treatment		
Capital expenditure treated as revenue expenditure	• Profit will be understated (losses will be overstated) • Non-current asset valuations will be understated (leading to possible errors in calculating depreciation)	*Example:* legal fees paid on the purchase of premises have been debited to an expense account
Revenue expenditure treated as capital expenditure	• Profit will be overstated (losses will be understated) • Non-current asset valuations will be overstated	*Example:* repairs to a motor vehicle have been debited to the motor vehicles account
Capital receipts treated as revenue receipts	• Profit will be overstated (losses will be understated)	*Example:* the proceeds from the sale of some equipment at net book value has been credited to the income statement
Revenue receipts treated as capital receipts	• Profit will be understated (losses will be overstated)	*Example:* interest received is credited to the investment account rather than an income account

◀◀ Recap

1. Incorrect treatment of capital and revenue expenditure will result in incorrect profits and asset valuations.

2. Incorrect treatment of capital and revenue receipts will result in incorrect profits.

✎ Apply

4. Yasmin has prepared her business's financial statements. They show a draft profit for the year of $38 000 and net current assets totalling $89 000.

   It appears that **i.** carriage inwards $1,000 relating to the purchase of some furniture was charged to the income statement and **ii.** the cost of maintaining computer equipment $2,000 was debited to the equipment account.

   Calculate corrected figures for **(a)** profit for the year, and **(b)** net non-current assets.

 Review

There are more details about the effect of the incorrect treatment of capital and revenue items on profit and asset valuations in section 4.5 of *Essential Accounting for Cambridge IGCSE® & O Level (third edition)*, pages 167–8.

- define depreciation
- explain the reasons for accounting for depreciation
- name and describe the straight-line, reducing-balance and revaluation methods of depreciation
- prepare ledger accounts and journal entries for the provision of depreciation, and how to record the sale of non-current assets, including the use of disposal accounts.

4.2.1 Depreciation: background

Non-current assets lose their value over time for a number of reasons:

Reason	Example
Usage (sometimes referred to as 'wear and tear')	A delivery vehicle will lose value the more it is used
Technological change causing a non-current asset to become out of date	Computers can become out of date when they are superseded by new versions
Inadequacy causing a non-current asset to cease to be useful as a business grows	A machine could no longer be of use if it cannot meet increased demand in an expanding business
Time factor some non-current assets have a fixed life	Shop premises held on a lease steadily lose value as the period of the lease expires
Depletion some non-current assets lose their value as resources are extracted	Mines, quarries and wells each lose value as resources are removed

Depreciation has a specific meaning: the loss in value of a non-current asset over its useful life. Almost all non-current assets are subject to depreciation (most forms of land are an exception).

Depreciation is an expense which is charged to the annual income statement. The term '**net book value**' is used to describe the value of a non-current asset based on cost less accumulated depreciation.

Methods of calculating depreciation

There are three main methods used to calculate depreciation:

1. The straight-line method of depreciation is sometimes called the fixed installment method. It is appropriate to use this method when a non-current asset is likely to benefit a business to the same extent each accounting year. It has the advantage of being easy to calculate. Residual value is a reference to the estimated value of the asset at the end of its useful life (sometimes called scrap value).

2. The reducing-balance method of depreciation is sometimes called the diminishing balance method. It is appropriate to use this method when it is likely that an asset will lose the most value in its first year and lose less value in each succeeding year. It is less easy to calculate as the depreciation charge is subject to a different calculation each year of the asset's life.

3. The revaluation method is useful where a non-current asset consists of many small items each of which may last a few years but which would be impractical (far too time consuming) to depreciate separately using either the straight-line or reducing-balance methods. The method is relatively easy to use but the figures used will be based on someone's opinion (i.e. subjective) rather than hard facts (i.e. objective).

Method	Description	Key feature
Straight-line	The annual depreciation charge is based on the original cost of the non-current asset (less any **residual value**) divided by the estimated years the asset will be of use in the business.	The annual depreciation charge is the same each year the asset is in use.
	Example: furniture cost $12 500, estimated residual value $700, expected useful life 5 years. *Depreciation per annum*: ⅕ × $11 800 = $2 360	
Reducing-balance	The annual depreciation charge is based on the value of the non-current asset at the beginning of the accounting year (the **net book value**).	The annual depreciation charge decreases each year the asset is in use.
	Example: motor vehicle cost $20 000 to be depreciated by 25% per annum. *Depreciation Year 1*: ¼ × $20 000 = $5 000 *Depreciation Year 2*: ¼ × net book value $15 000 = $3 750	
Revaluation	The annual depreciation charge is based on comparing the value of the asset at the end of the accounting year with its value at the beginning of the year.	The annual depreciation charge varies from year to year.
	Example: a hotel valued its bedding at $8 200 on 1 January, purchased new bedding at $2 300 during the year, and valued the bedding at $8 900 on 31 December. *Depreciation charge for the year*: opening value + additions ($8 200 + $2 300 = $10 500) less closing value $8 900 = $1 600	

Depreciation and accounting principles

Depreciation is a good example of the matching (accruals) concept, which requires the revenue of an accounting period to be matched with all the costs incurred in achieving that revenue.

The consistency principle is also applied to depreciation. It requires the same depreciation method to be used each year. As a result, it is possible to make valid comparisons of a business's results, comparing one year with another.

Exam tip

There is more detailed coverage of accounting principles in Unit 7.

◀◀ **Recap**

1. Non-current assets lose their value over their useful lives for a variety of reasons, of which wear and tear is the most common.

2. There are three main methods of calculating depreciation, each of which results in providing an estimate of the loss in value of the non-current asset during a year.

3. Depreciation is charged to the income statement each year.

4. Depreciation is required in order to comply with the matching (accruals) principle.

5. The same depreciation method should be applied each year in order to comply with the consistency principle.

Apply

1. Candy purchased some office equipment on 1 January 2018 for $18 000. Candy's financial year ends on 31 December. She expects the equipment to be in use for four years and to have a final residual value of $1,600.

   (a) Calculate the annual depreciation charge using the straight-line method.

   (b) Calculate the net book value of the office equipment at the end of 2019.

2. Abdul purchased a delivery vehicle on 1 January 2018 for $32 000. He has decided to depreciate the motor vehicle by 25 per cent per annum using the reducing-balance method. Abdul's financial year ends on 31 December. Calculate the depreciation to be charged to the income statement at the end of:

   (a) 2018

   (b) 2019.

3. Asif owns a café. The small items of kitchen equipment are depreciated using the revaluation method. On 1 January 2018 small items of kitchen equipment had a value of $8,900. During the year ended 31 December 2018 he purchased additional small items of kitchen equipment for $1,700. At 31 December 2018 he valued the small items of kitchen equipment at $9,200. Calculate the depreciation charge for 2018.

Review

There is more about the background to depreciation and illustrations of depreciation calculations in sections 4.6 and 4.7 of *Essential Accounting for Cambridge IGCSE® & O Level (third edition)*, pages 172–4.

4.2.2 Ledger and journal entries to record depreciation

Each class of non-current assets requires two ledger accounts.

Ledger account	Typical entries
Equipment at cost account	Debit: purchase of the non-current asset
	Debit: additional purchases of non-current assets
	Credit: the cost of any of the non-current assets when sold
Provision for depreciation of equipment account	Credit: the depreciation charge for each year

Entries when purchasing a non-current asset

Transaction	Book of prime entry	Debit	Credit
Cash purchase of a non-current asset	Cash book	Non-current asset at cost account	Bank
Purchase of a non-current asset on credit	General journal	Non-current asset at cost account	Supplier's account

Entries when depreciating a non-current asset

Book of prime entry	Debit	Credit
General journal	Income statement	Provision for depreciation of a non-current asset

Provision for depreciation account

Example:

Provision for depreciation of equipment account							
Year 1			$	Year 1			$
Dec	31	Balance c/d	3 000	Dec	31	Income statement	3 000
Year 2				Year 2			
Dec	31	Balance c/d	6 000	Jan	1	Balance b/d	3 000
				Dec	31	Income statement	3 000
			6 000				6 000
Year 3				Year 3			
Dec	31	Balance c/d	9 000	Jan	1	Balance b/d	6 000
				Dec	31	Income statement	3 000
			9 000				9 000
				Year 4			
				Jan	1	Balance b/d	9 000

The example above illustrates entries where the straight-line method of depreciation has been used. It is assumed the equipment cost $30 000 and is being depreciated by 10 per cent per annum. The year end is assumed to be 31 December.

Each year on 31 December an entry will be made in the general journal to record the transfer of depreciation to the income statement. Each year on 31 December the account should be balanced, and the balance brought down to the credit side of the account.

The provision account records the steadily accumulating figure for depreciation.

> **Exam tip**
>
> A common mistake is to omit the year in the date column on both the debit side and credit side of the account. This must be checked throughout the account.

Depreciation and the statement of financial position

The statement of financial position should record:

- the original cost of each type of non-current asset
- the accumulated provision for depreciation at the date of the statement
- the net book value of each type of non-current asset.

Exam tip

A common error is to record only the current year's depreciation on the statement of financial position. The accumulated depreciation charge should be shown.

Statement of financial position at 31 December 2019 (Extract)			
	$	$	$
	Cost	Accumulated depreciation	Net
Non-current assets			
Motor vehicles	75 000	42 000	33 000
Furniture and fittings	12 000	4 800	7 200
	87 000	46 800	40 200

Recap

1. Separate ledger accounts are maintained to record the cost of each non-current asset and the provision for depreciation of each non-current asset.

2. The provision for depreciation account records the annual depreciation charge and the balance of the account represents the steadily accumulating total of depreciation on that type of non-current asset.

3. The general journal is used to record the purchase of a non-current asset on credit and the transfer of the annual depreciation charges to the income statement.

4. The statement of financial position should record for each type of non-current asset: the cost, the accumulating depreciation and the net book value.

Apply

4. The owner of a business purchased some machinery on credit on 1 January 2018 from W Limited. The machinery cost $38 000. The machinery is to be depreciated using the straight-line method; it is expected to have a useful life of four years and have a residual value of $3,200. Prepare journal entries (including narratives) to record, for the year ended 31 December 2018:

   (a) the purchase of the machinery

   (b) the transfer of the annual depreciation charge to the income statement.

5. Asif uses the reducing-balance method at a rate of 30 per cent per annum to depreciate his motor vehicles. The motor vehicles were purchased for $50 000 on 1 January 2016. The business's year end is 31 December. Prepare:

   (a) the provision for depreciation of motor vehicles account for each of the years 2016, 2017 and 2018

   (b) an extract from the business's statement of financial position at 31 December 2017 to show motor vehicles.

 **Review**

There is more about recording depreciation in sections 4.8 and 4.9 of *Essential Accounting for Cambridge IGCSE® & O Level (third edition)*, pages 175–7.

4.2.3 The disposal of a non-current asset

Details of the disposal of a non-current asset are recorded in a separate nominal ledger account. The account is designed to show any profit or loss arising from the disposal.

A profit on disposal will arise when depreciation charges have been overestimated. A loss on disposal will arise when depreciation charges have been underestimated.

The following steps are required when a non-current asset is sold:

Step	Transaction	Book of prime entry	Double-entry details
1	Transfer the cost of the non-current asset to the disposal account	General journal	Dr Disposal account Cr Non-current asset account
2	Transfer the accumulated depreciation on the non-current asset from the provision for depreciation account	General journal	Dr Provision for depreciation account Cr Disposal account
3	Record the proceeds from the sale of the non-current asset	Cash book	Dr Bank Cr Disposal account
4	Balance the disposal account and transfer the profit or loss on disposal to the income statement (entries made at the year end)	General journal	If a profit: Dr Disposal account Cr Income statement If a loss: Dr Income statement Cr Disposal account

The example below looks at the disposal of some equipment which cost $10 000 and on which there was accumulated depreciation of $7,500.

1. Where a profit is made on disposal (the equipment is sold for $3,800):

Disposal account			
	$		$
Equipment (cost)	10 000	Provision for depreciation	7 500
Income statement	1 300	Bank	3 800
	11 300		11 300

2. Where a loss is made on disposal (the equipment is sold for $1,900):

Disposal account			
	$		$
Equipment (cost)	10 000	Provision for depreciation	7 500
		Bank	1 900
		Income statement	600
	10 000		10 000

Recap

1. The details of the disposal of a non-current asset are recorded in a separate ledger account.

2. On the date of the disposal the account should record the original cost of the asset, accumulated depreciation and the sale proceeds.

3. At the year end the balance of the account should be transferred to the income statement. The balance will represent either a profit or a loss on the disposal.

Apply

6. The owner of a business sold a delivery vehicle on 15 April 2018. The following details are available: delivery vehicle had cost $27 500; accumulated depreciation $22 800; sale proceeds $3,200. Prepare:

   (a) the entries in the general journal to record the disposal (include narratives)

   (b) the disposal account including dates (balance the account on 31 December 2018).

Review

There is more about the disposal of non-current assets in section 4.10 of *Essential Accounting for Cambridge IGCSE® & O Level (third edition)*, pages 178–80.

- recognize the importance of matching costs and revenues
- prepare ledger accounts and journal entries to record accrued and prepaid expenses and incomes.

4.3.1 Expense adjustments

The importance of matching costs and revenues

There is a precise rule for how profits should be calculated. The rule requires the revenues for a period to be matched against all the costs which have arisen during that period.

This rule is referred to as the **matching principle**. It is sometimes also called the accruals principle. An accounting period is usually a year.

Revenues for a period refers to sales and other sources of income (rent received, interest received, etc.). The amount recorded will be exactly for that period whether the money has been received or not. It will include any amounts due for the period not yet received, but exclude amounts already received but which are for the next period.

Costs for a period refer to all the expenses which have been incurred in order to achieve the revenue and other incomes. The amount recorded will be the appropriate amount for the period, whether the money has actually been paid or not. The amount will include any amounts due for the period but not yet paid, but exclude any amounts paid which relate to the next accounting period.

This rule ensures all organizations calculate their profits (or losses) in the same way. As a result, it is possible to make meaningful comparisons of a business's performance with previous years or with other similar businesses.

> **Exam tip**
>
> There is more about the matching principle in Unit 7.

Recording accrued expenses

Where an expense remains unpaid for part of an accounting period, the amount due is referred to as an accrual and reference is made to an **accrued expense**.

The amount unpaid has to be included in the amount recorded for that expense in the income statement for that accounting period.

The accrued expense is also shown on the organization's statement of financial position as a current liability and is labelled '**other payable**'.

Here is an expense account before recording an accrual:

Expense account				
2018		$		$
Jan-Dec	Bank	14 000		

The account after recording the accrual and transfer to the income statement would look like this:

Expense account							
2018			$	2018			$
Jan-Dec		Bank	14 000	**Dec**	**31**	**Income statement**	**14 400**
Dec	**31**	**Balance c/d**	**400**				
			14 400				14 400
				2019			
				Jan	**1**	**Balance b/d**	**400**

Exam tip

It is important to balance accounts and bring the balances down. Dates (including years) should be shown.

Although only $14 000 has been paid for this expense during the year, the transfer to the income statement included an amount unpaid of $400 at the year end.

The account should be balanced at the year end and the balance brought down to the credit side as the accrued expense is a liability.

The transfer to the income statement should appear first as an entry in the general journal:

Journal				Dr	Cr
2018				$	$
Dec	31	Income statement		14 400	
		Expense account			14 400
		Transfer of expense to the income statement			

Recording prepaid expenses

Where payment for an expense covers part of the next accounting period it is referred to as a prepayment and reference is made to an **expense prepaid**.

The amount prepaid must be excluded from that accounting period's income statement. The amount is shown on the organization's statement of financial position as a current asset and labelled '**other receivable**'.

Here is an example of an expense account before recording a prepayment:

Expense account				
2018		$		$
Jan-Dec	Bank	23 900		

The account after recording the accrual and transfer to the income statement would look like this:

Expense account					
2018		$	2018		$
Jan-Dec	Bank	23 900	Dec 31	Income statement	14 100
				Balance c/d	800
		23 900			23 900
2019					
Jan 1	Balance b/d	800			

Although $23 900 has been paid for this expense during the year, the transfer to the income statement is for just $14 100. The transfer excludes the amount of $800 prepaid for 2019.

The account should be balanced at the year end and the balance brought down to the debit side as the prepaid expense is an asset.

The transfer to the income statement should appear first as an entry in the general journal.

Exam tip

Avoid abbreviating the word 'balance'.

Working out time spans

Often, making adjustments requires calculations to be made of the time between two dates. To become skilful in this task it can help to sketch out a timescale, as shown below.

2017		2018												2019		
Nov	Dec	Jan	Feb	Mar	Apr	May	June	July	Aug	Sept	Oct	Nov	Dec	Jan	Feb	Mar

The timescale can start and end wherever is most suitable for the situation under review.

Using the example above it becomes relatively easy to see how many months there are between 1 June 2018 and 28 February 2019:

2017		2018												2019		
Nov	Dec	Jan	Feb	Mar	Apr	May	**June**	July	Aug	Sept	Oct	Nov	Dec	Jan	**Feb**	Mar

Exam tip

When using a timescale chart, double-check whether the beginning date is for the first of the month or the end of the month, and check whether the end date is for the beginning or end of a month.

Expense accounts with opening balances

Expense accounts may start with opening balances for an accrual or prepayment brought down from the previous year.

The example below shows an accrued expense as an opening and closing balance:

Expense account							
2018			$	2018			$
Jan-Dec	Bank		11 900	**Jan**	**1**	**Balance b/d**	**720**
Dec	**31**	**Balance c/d**	**910**	Dec	31	Income statement	12 090
			12 810				12 810
				2019			
				Jan	1	Balance b/d	910

The expense account starts with an opening credit balance of $720, which represents the amount owed or the previous year (2017). The amount transferred to the income statement represents the business's expense for 2018. Therefore it excludes the amount owed for 2017, but includes the amount due at the end of 2018.

The example below shows a prepaid expense as an opening and closing balance:

Expense account						
2018			$	2018		$
Jan	**1**	**Balance b/d**	**360**	Dec	31	Income statement	8 330
Jan-Dec		Bank	8 210			Balance c/d	240
			8 570				8 570
2019						
Jan	1	Balance b/d	240			

The expense account starts with an opening debit balance of $360, which represents the amount prepaid in the previous year (2017).

The amount transferred to the income statement represents the business's expense for 2018. Therefore it includes the opening prepayment, but excludes the amount prepaid for 2019.

Accounts combining two expenses

In some cases it may be convenient for a business to use one ledger account for a combination of expenses. The account could show:

- two opening balances – a prepayment for one of the expenses and an accrual for the other expense

- payments made for each type of expense

- a single figure for the transfer to the income statement combining the annual costs for each expense

- two closing balance to carry down – a prepayment for one of the expenses and an accrual for the other expense.

Stationery and computer supplies account					
2018		$	2018		$
Jan 1	Balance b/d (stationery)	360	Jan 1	Balance b/d (computer supplies)	330
Jan-Dec	Bank (stationery)	1 290	Dec 31	Income statement	4 260
	Bank (computer supplies)	2 820		Balance c/d	170
Dec 31	Balance c/d	290			
		4 760			4 760
2019			2019		
Jan 1	Balance b/d (stationery)	170	Jan 1	Balance b/d (computer supplies)	290

The single figure transfer to the income statement has been entered as the balancing figure in the account after all the other entries have been made.

The income statement transfer can also be calculated as follows:

- stationery $1,480 ($360 opening prepayment + $1,290 bank – $170 closing prepayment)

- computer supplies $2,780 ($2,820 bank – opening accrual $330 + closing accrual $290)

- total: stationery $1,480 + computer supplies $2,780 = $4,260.

Apply

1. Morad made the following expense payments during his business's most recent financial year: wages $23 450, carriage outwards $1,190. At the year end the following amounts were due but unpaid: wages $3,340, carriage outwards $230. State the amount to be transferred to the business's income statement for:

   (a) wages   (b) carriage outwards.

2. Kate made the following expense payments during her business's most recent financial year: insurance $4,920, rent $13 450. At the year end the following amounts were prepaid: insurance $350, rent $990. State the amount to be transferred to the business's income statement for:

   (a) insurance   (b) rent.

3. On 1 November 2018 a business paid insurance for the period 1 November 2018 to 30 June 2019. State how many months of insurance had been prepaid, assuming the business's financial year end is:

   (a) 28 February 2019   (b) 31 March 2019.

4. A business's financial year end is 30 September. No payment had been made for some expenses as follows: electricity charges for period beginning 1 May, interest for period beginning 1 August. State how many months had been unpaid for:

   (a) electricity

   (b) interest at the business's financial year end.

Recap

1. A business's profit or loss is based on matching revenues and other incomes for a period with the expenses for the same period, whether or not the amounts have actually been received or paid.

2. The transfer to the income statement for an expense should take account of any amounts unpaid for the period concerned. These unpaid amounts are referred to as accruals.

3. The transfer to the income statement for an expense should exclude any amount paid for another accounting period. These amounts are referred to as prepayments.

4. Accrued expenses appear as credit balances, whereas prepayments appear as debit balances.

5. Accrued expenses are current liabilities (other payables); prepaid expenses are current assets (other receivables).

6. Expense accounts may have opening balances representing a prepayment (debit balance) or accrual (credit balance).

7. Sometimes one expense account may be used to record entries for two similar types of expense.

Review

There is more about the background to expense adjustments in section 4.11 of *Essential Accounting for Cambridge IGCSE® & O Level (third edition)*, pages 186–7.

4.3.2 Income adjustments

When the matching principle is applied to income items the entries shown below are required.

Accrued income at the year end

Here is an income account before recording the accrued income:

Income account			
	$	2018	$
		Jan-Dec Bank	11 300

The account after recording the accrued income and transfer to the income statement would look like this:

Income account					
2018		$	2018		$
Dec	31	Income statement	11 800	Jan-Dec Bank	11 300
				Dec 31 **Balance c/d**	**500**
			11 800		**11 800**
2019					
Jan	**1**	**Balance b/d**	**500**		

Although $11 300 has actually been received during the year, the amount transferred to the income statement is $11 800, in order to take account of the accrued income.

Accrued income appears as a debit balance in the income account as it is an asset.

Accrued income is shown as a current asset (other receivables) on a statement of financial position.

The transfer to the income statement should first be recorded in the general journal:

Journal				Dr	Cr
				$	$
2018					
Dec	31	Income account		11 800	
		Income statement			11 800
		Transfer of income to the income statement			

Prepaid income at the year end

Here is an income account before recording the prepaid income:

	$	2018		$
		Jan-Dec	Bank	7 800

Income account

The account after recording the accrued income and transfer to the income statement would look like this:

Income account

2018			$	2018			$
Dec	31	Income statement	7 400	Jan-Dec		Bank	7 800
		Balance c/d	400				
			7 800				7 800
				2019			
				Jan	1	Balance b/d	400

Although $7,800 has actually been received during the year, the amount transferred to the income statement is $7,400, which ensures the income prepaid is excluded.

Prepaid income appears as a credit balance in the income account as it is a liability. Prepaid income is shown as a current liability on a statement of financial position.

The transfer to the income statement should first be recorded in the general journal.

Income accounts with opening balances

If income accounts show closing balances for accrued and/or prepaid income, it follows that the following year will begin with those items as opening balances.

This income account shows accrued income as an opening and closing balance:

Income account

2018			$	2018			$
Jan	1	Balance b/d	300	Jan-Dec		Bank	6 100
Dec	31	Income statement	6 200	Dec	31	Balance c/d	400
			6 500				6 500
2019							
Jan	1	Balance b/d	400				

The income account starts with an opening balance of $300, which represents the amount due for the previous year (2017).

The amount transferred to the income statement represents the business's income for 2018. Therefore it excludes the amount due for 2017, but includes the closing accrued income.

This income account shows prepaid income as an opening and closing balance:

Income account						
2018			$	2018		$
Dec	31	Income statement	8 980	Jan 1	Balance b/d	350
		Balance c/d	520	Jan-Dec	Bank	9 150
			9 500			9 500
				2019		
				Jan 1	Balance b/d	520

The income account starts with an opening balance of $350, which represents income prepaid in the previous year (2017).

The amount transferred to the income statement represents the business's income for 2018. Therefore it includes the opening prepaid income, but excludes the closing prepaid income.

Recap

1. An income account must be adjusted if there is accrued income or prepaid income at the year end, so that only the income for the period under review is transferred to the income statement.

2. Accrued income appears as a debit balance and as a current asset (account receivable) in a statement of financial position.

3. Prepaid income appears as a credit balance and as a current liability (account payable) in a statement of financial position.

4. Income accounts may start with opening balances representing accrued income (debit balance) or prepaid income (credit balance) brought down from the previous year.

Apply

5. Antonia has received the following amounts from two sources of income during a recent financial year: rent received $11 900, interest received $4,250. At the end of the financial year accrued rent received is $530 and prepaid interest received is $110. State how much should be transferred to the business's income statement for the year under review for:

   (a) rent received

   (b) interest received.

6. A business's accounting year ends on 31 October. During the year ended 31 October 2018 the business had received $2,300 in interest. Interest amount at $220 per month had not been received for the period 1 August to 31 October. State:

   (a) the amount of interest received to be shown in the income statement for the year ended 31 October 2018

   (b) how the amount of interest receivable should be shown in the statement of financial position at 31 October 2018.

7. A business's rent received account had a debit balance of $640 on 1 January 2018. During the year ended 31 December 2018 the business received $7,830 in rent. At 31 December 2018 rent of $730 had been received in advance for 2019. State:

   (a) how much rent received should appear in the business's income statement for the year ended 31 December 2018

   (b) how rent receivable should appear on the business's statement of financial position at 31 December 2018.

Review

There is more about the background to income adjustments in section 4.12 of *Essential Accounting for Cambridge IGCSE® & O Level (third edition)*, pages 188–9.

You will need to know how to:

- explain the meaning of irrecoverable debts and recovery of debts written off
- prepare ledger accounts and journal entries to record irrecoverable debts
- prepare ledger accounts and journal entries to record recovery of debts written off
- explain the reasons for maintaining provisions for doubtful debts
- prepare ledger accounts and journal entries to record the creation of, and adjustments to, a provision for doubtful debts.

4.4.1 Irrecoverable debts and recovery of debts written off

Term	What the term means	Why does this happen?
Irrecoverable debt	An amount due from a credit customer which is not going to be paid, resulting in an expense.	The credit customer may have: • no funds to pay • gone out of business • moved away and cannot be found.
Recovery of debts written off	Where a credit customer pays all (or some) of the amount due after the debt has been written off, resulting in income for a business.	The credit customer may: • now have the funds available to pay • wish to restore good relationships with the business.

Avoiding irrecoverable debts and credit control

When a new customer asks for credit terms, check with the customer's bank and that customer's suppliers to establish whether the person or organization is creditworthy.

Set a credit limit for each customer – this will be low in the case of new customers and higher in the case of those customers who have proved to be reliable.

Maintain detailed records of how much each customer owes and for how long the debt has been outstanding (sometimes referred to as an **aging schedule of trade receivables**).

You can also:

- act promptly when sending out invoices, statements of account and reminders
- offer cash discounts to encourage early settlement of the amount due
- charge interest on overdue accounts as a way of motivating customers to pay on time.

Recap

1. Irrecoverable debts represent a loss to a business. They should be identified as quickly as possible and recorded.

2. Occasionally, a credit customer will pay the amount due after the sales ledger account has been written off.

3. Businesses can try to minimize the chances of irrecoverable debts arising by employing strict credit limits.

Apply

1. Kai sold goods on credit (worth $1,480) to Ace Retail Stores in October 2017. In March 2018 it became clear that the amount due from Ace Retail Stores would not be paid, and the account was written off as irrecoverable on 28 March 2018. State two reasons why Ace Retail Stores may have failed to pay the amount owed to Kai.

2. Kai is hoping to avoid irrecoverable debts in future, and has considered offering credit customers a cash discount. Describe how offering a cash discount could help avoid the occurrence of irrecoverable debts.

Review

There are more details about irrecoverable debts and recovery of debts written off in section 4.15 of *Essential Accounting for Cambridge IGCSE® & O Level (third edition)*, pages 196–7.

4.4.2 Recording irrecoverable debts

Step 1	Journal entry
Step 2	Dr Irrecoverable debts
	Cr Trade receivables
Step 3	Transfer irrecoverable debts to the income statement at the end of the year as an expense
	Close trade receivable account

Recap

Irrecoverable debts should be written off promptly. This requires an entry in the general journal and the closure of the credit customer's account.

 **Apply**

3. Return to Kai and the irrecoverable debt.

    (a) Prepare an entry in the journal to record the irrecoverable debt on 28 March 2018.

    (b) Prepare the following accounts in Kai's books: Ace Retail Stores, irrecoverable debts.

Review

There is a full illustration of writing off an irrecoverable debt in section 4.15 of *Essential Accounting for Cambridge IGCSE® & O Level (third edition)*, page 196.

4.4.3 Recording recovery of debts written off

Step 1	Journal entry
Step 2	Dr Trade receivable
	Cr Recovery of debts written off
Step 3	Cash book
Step 4	Dr Bank
	Cr Trade receivable
Step 5	Close trade receivable account
	Transfer recovery of debts written off to the income statement as income

It is common practice to reinstate the account of the trade receivable when recovery of a debt written off occurs. Recording the recovery of debts written off requires a journal entry.

 Recap

When a debt previously written off is recovered, it is usual to reinstate the account of the trade receivable and then close the account with the receipt of the amount due. The amount recovered is regarded as income.

✎ Apply

4. Return to Kai and the irrecoverable debt. On 3 December 2018, Ace Retail Stores sent a cheque for $1,480 to Kai.

    (a) Prepare the following account in Kai's books: recovery of debts written off.

    (b) State how the balance of the irrecoverable debts account and the recovery of debts written off account will be treated in Kai's end-of-year financial statements.

⏱ Review

There is full illustration of recording an irrecoverable debt recovered in section 4.15 of *Essential Accounting for Cambridge IGCSE® & O Level (third edition)*, page 197.

4.4.4 Provision for doubtful debts

A **provision for doubtful debts** is the amount of profit set aside to cover any outstanding debts which are not likely to be paid and so will become irrecoverable.

Purpose	To ensure profits are not overstated and trade receivables are recorded at a **true and fair** value on the statement of financial position.
Accounting principles	• Prudence: ensuring profits and asset values are not overstated.
	• Matching (accruals): ensuring profits are based on matching the credit sales for a year with the likely irrecoverable debts.
Basis for the percentage used for the provision	• Based on past experience of the likelihood of irrecoverable debts and the current economic climate.
	• Using an aging schedule of trade receivables, where the older the debt is, the greater the risk that it could become irrecoverable.

Recap

1. A provision for doubtful debts account always has a credit balance.

2. When a provision is created, profits are reduced in the income statement.

3. In subsequent years, the provision should be increased (or decreased) if there is an increase (or decrease) in total trade receivables and profits reduced.

Apply

5. Explain why it is important for a business which has credit sales to consider creating a provision for doubtful debts.

Review

There is further information about provisions for doubtful debts in section 4.16 of *Essential Accounting for Cambridge IGCSE® & O Level (third edition)*, pages 198–200.

4.4.5 Recording provision for doubtful debts

Creating a provision for doubtful debts

Step 1	Information needed at year end	Trade receivables
		Percentage chosen for the provision
Step 2	Journal entry	Dr Income statement
		Cr Provision for doubtful debts account
Step 3	Nominal ledger	Prepare a provision for doubtful debts account and credit the account with the amount of the provision
Step 4	Income statement	Enter the provision in the second part of the income statement as an expense
Step 5	Statement of financial position	Record total trade receivables less provision for doubtful debts to show a net figure

Adjusting a provision for doubtful debts

Once a provision has been created, it has to be adjusted at the end of each financial year to keep it in step with the total of trade receivables.

Step 1	Information needed at year end	• Latest figure for total trade receivables
		• Percentage chosen for the provision
Step 2	Calculate the amount of any adjustment required	• Compare the existing provision with the provision now required
Step 3 (if the provision needs to be INCREASED)		
Journal entry		Dr Income statement
		Cr Provision for doubtful debts account
Nominal ledger		Cr the provision account with the amount of the increase in the provision
Income statement		Enter the amount of the increase in the provision in the second part of the income statement as an expense
Statement of financial position		Record total trade receivables less the updated provision for doubtful debts to show a net figure
Step 3 (if the provision needs to be DECREASED)		
Journal entry		Dr Provision for doubtful debts
		Cr Income statement
Nominal ledger		Dr the provision account with the amount of the decrease in the provision
Income statement		Enter the amount of the decrease in the provision in the second part of the income statement as income
Statement of financial position		Record total trade receivables less the updated provision for doubtful debts to show a net figure

Exam tip

In the statement of financial position, set out the details of the trade receivables and the provision for doubtful debts – not just the net figure.

Common errors

In the years after a provision for doubtful debts has been created, a common mistake is to record the total provision for doubtful debts in an income statement, rather than just the amount of any adjustment.

Format for a provision for doubtful debts account

Dr				Provision for doubtful debts				Cr
			$					$
Year 2				Year 1				
Dec	31	Balance c/d	xxx	Dec	31	Income statement		xxx
				Year 2				
				Dec	31	Income statement		xxx
			xxx					xxx
Year 3				Year 3				
Dec	31	Income statement	xxx	Jan	1	Balance b/d		xxx
	31	Balance c/d	xxx					
			xxx					xxx
				Year 4				
				Jan	1	Balance b/d		xxx

The example above shows the provision account over a four-year period:

- Year 1: the provision is created.
- Year 2: the provision is increased and the account is balanced.
- Year 3: the provision is decreased and the account is balanced.
- Year 4: the account balance is brought down to start the year.

Recap

1. Provisions for doubtful debts are first recorded in the general journal.
2. A provision account always has a credit balance.
3. Increases in a provision are credited to the account.
4. Decreases in a provision are debited to the account.

Apply

6. A business has a provision for doubtful debts of $1,240. On 31 December 2018 the business trade receivables totalled $28 800. It has been decided to maintain the provision for doubtful debts at 4 per cent of trade receivables. Prepare the provision for doubtful debts account for 2018.

Review

There are further details about recording provisions for doubtful debts in sections 4.16 and 4.17 of *Essential Accounting for Cambridge IGCSE® & O Level (third edition)*, pages 198–203.

- understand the basis of the valuation of inventory
- prepare simple inventory valuation statements
- recognize the importance of valuation of inventory and the effect of an incorrect valuation on gross profit, profit for the year, equity and asset valuation.

4.5.1 The rule for the valuation of inventory

The rule for valuing inventory is that inventory is valued at the cost or net realizable value – whichever is lower. Inventory is valued at cost in accordance with the historic cost principle (which ensures objectivity rather than opinion is the basis for valuing assets).

Net realizable value is used in accordance with the prudence principle to ensure, where there is doubt, asset values and profits are not overstated. Realizable value is the accounting term used for turning something into cash (in this case, selling inventory).

Net realizable value means the resale value less any costs incurred in putting inventory in a saleable condition (perhaps repairing an item which has been damaged).

Applying the rule for the valuation of inventory

When valuing inventory at the end of a financial year most, if not all items, will be valued at cost. However, for example, where there are items in the storeroom which are at risk of not being sold because they are no longer in demand or have become damaged, then their value will need careful assessment.

A business is valuing inventory at the financial year end. Two items (A and B) have become slightly damaged. The following steps have been taken:

Step		Item A	Item B
1	Check the cost of the item	Cost $30	Cost $42
2	Check the normal selling price of the item (i.e. the realizable value)	Realizable value $36	Realizable value $50
3	Estimate the cost of putting the item in a saleable condition	$7	$5
4	Calculate the net realizable value (NRV)	NRV $36 – $7 = $29	$50 – $5 = $45
5	Decide which is lower: cost or NRV	Cost $30 or NRV $29	Cost $42 or NRV $45
6	State the valuation for the inventory	$29 (NRV)	$42 (cost)

Preparing an inventory valuation statement

Details of inventory items can be set out in the form of a table:

Statement of inventory valuation at (date)				
Inventory item	Number of items	Cost	NRV	Total value
		$	$	$
XB2	30	42	40	1 200
YH4	25	27	29	675
ZT3	11	57	54	594
Total				2 469

For each item the valuation has been based on cost or NRV – whichever is the lower:

- XB2 items have been valued at NRV.

- YH4 items have been valued at cost.

- ZT3 items have been valued at NRV.

 Recap

1. Inventory should be valued at the lower of cost or net realizable value (NRV).

2. The rule for valuing inventory is an example of the application of the accounting principle of prudence.

3. In order to value inventory it is necessary to consider: the cost of the item, the sale value (realizable value), the costs if any which will need to be incurred in order to put the item in a saleable condition.

4. The rule is required when inventory has become damaged or no longer in demand and at risk of not being sold unless its selling price is reduced.

Apply

1. Sanath has been checking his business's inventory. There is one item in the storeroom which cost $480 but which has been slightly damaged. This item would normally be sold for $560. Sanath has received an estimate of $90 for repairing the damage to this item. How should this item be valued?

2. Ravi was valuing his business's inventory at the end of the financial year. There were 20 damaged items in the storeroom which cost $25 each. These items would normally be sold at $31 each but will require $8 each to be spent on minor repairs. Calculate the total value of these items.

Review

There is more about the valuation of inventories in section 4.3 of *Essential Accounting for Cambridge IGCSE® & O Level (third edition)*, pages 160–1.

Exam tip

There is more detailed coverage of accounting principles of historic cost and prudence in Unit 7.

4.5.2 The effects of an incorrect valuation of inventory

When inventory is valued incorrectly it sets off a chain reaction of incorrect figures in the financial statements. Since one year's closing inventory becomes the next year's opening inventory, it follows that an incorrect valuation of closing inventory will affect key figures in the financial statements for two consecutive years.

	Closing inventory valuation		Opening inventory valuation	
	Too high	*Too low*	*Too high*	*Too low*
Cost of sales	Understated	Overstated	Overstated	Understated
Gross profit	Overstated	Understated	Understated	Overstated
Profit for the year	Overstated	Understated	Understated	Overstated
Current assets subtotal at year end	Overstated	Understated	Not affected	Not affected
Capital subtotal at year end	Overstated	Understated	Understated	Overstated

 Recap

1. Any error in the valuation of inventory will have many consequences for figures in the financial statements.

2. An incorrect valuation will mean that cost of sales, gross profit and profit for the year will be incorrectly recorded in the income statement.

3. An incorrect valuation will mean that current assets and capital will be incorrectly recorded in the income statement.

Apply

3. Kai has prepared an income statement which records a gross profit of $85 000 and a profit for the year of $27 000. However, he has now noticed that his closing inventory was undervalued by $2,000. State the corrected figure for:

   (a) gross profit

   (b) profit for the year.

4. Maria has prepared a statement of financial position which includes a figure of $31 000 for current assets, a loss for the year of $6,300 and a closing capital of $108 200. Maria has made an error in valuing the closing inventory. The inventory was overvalued by $3 200. State corrected figures for:

   (a) current assets

   (b) loss for the year

   (c) closing capital.

Review

There is more about the effects of incorrect inventory valuation in section 4.3 of *Essential Accounting for Cambridge IGCSE® & O Level (third edition)*, pages 160–1.

Exam-style questions

1. Khalid, a retailer, decided to open a new branch in 2018. During the year ended 31 December 2018 the following transactions occurred relating to the new branch:

	$
Borrowed from the bank on a ten-year loan	24 000
Purchased shop premises	38 000
Paid to upgrade shop premises prior to opening	8 000
Paid interest on the bank loan	1 800
Sublet part of the shop premises and received rent from the tenant	3 500
Khalid invested more in the business from private resources	15 000
Paid legal fees in connection with the purchases of the shop premises	4 000

State what is meant by each of the following terms. In each case identify **one** example from the list of transactions:

(a) revenue expenditure (2)

(b) capital expenditure (2)

(c) revenue receipt (2)

(d) capital receipt. (2)

Additional information:

• Khalid debited the shop premises account with $38 000 as a result of the transactions listed above.

• Khalid's policy is to depreciate premises by 2.5 per cent per annum.

(e) Assess the effect of valuing the premises at $38 000 on the business's income statement for the year ended 31 December 2018 and the statement of financial position at that date. (5)

(Total marks: 13)

Before you answer the question

Look through the list of transactions and identify what type of expenditure and receipt is represented by each item.

Decide how much you think the new shop premises are worth.

Exam tip

To increase your confidence in this topic, spend time correcting your answer. Make sure you understand the nature of any mistakes you made, and write in corrections so that you have a final version of your answer which is totally correct.

Check your answer

1. **(a)** Revenue expenditure: money spent on the everyday running costs of a business. **(1)**

   Example: interest on bank loan. **(1)**

   (b) Capital expenditure: money spent on non-current assets including improvements to non-current assets. **(1)**

   Example: purchase of shop premises; upgrade to shop premises; legal fees paid in connection with purchase of shop premises. **(1)**

   (c) Revenue receipt: money received for normal business activities. **(1)**

   Example: rent received from subtenant. **(1)**

   (d) Capital receipt: money received from one-off non-trading activities. **(1)**

   Example: ten-year bank loan/additional investment in the business by Khalid. **(1)**

   (e) Khalid has understated the value of the shop premises by $12 000 **(1)** (i.e. the cost of the upgrade plus the legal fees paid in connection with the purchases of the shop premises). As a result, non-current assets will be understated **(1)** on the business's statement of financial position at 31 December 2018. In addition, depreciation on the shop premises will have been miscalculated **(1)**; it should have been $300 more **(1)** (i.e. 2.5% × $12 000) and therefore profit for the year ended 31 December 2018 will have been overstated **(1)**.

⊗ Common errors

Remember to:

- identify a correct example for each term
- identify a correct example selected from the list of transactions
- provide figures representing the inaccurate value of the premises in **(e)**
- notice that depreciation of the premises will have been incorrectly calculated for the year in **(e)**.

2. Salma owns a business making garments for the fashion industry. During the period 1 January 2016 to 31 December 2018 the business owned three machines as follows:

Machine	Purchase date	Cost
M1	1 January 2016	$24 000
M2	1 January 2017	$28 000
M3	1 July 2018	$20 000

Machines are purchased on credit from K Limited.

On 1 April 2018 machine 1 (M1) was sold for £12 300.

The business's accounting year end is 31 December.

Salma's policy is to depreciate machinery by 20 per cent per annum using the straight-line method. Depreciation is provided in the year of purchase based on the number of months the machine is owned by the business. No depreciation is charged in the year of sale.

(a) Prepare a journal entry and narrative to record the purchase of machine 2 (M2). **(3)**

(b) Prepare the following accounts for the years 2016, 2017 and 2018:

    i. machinery at cost account **(6)**

    ii. provision for depreciation of machinery account. **(6)**

(c) Calculate the profit or loss made on the disposal of M1. **(4)**

(Total marks: 19)

Before you answer the question

Check that you have noticed the dates on which key events occur.

Check that you are clear about the business's depreciation policy.

Remember that it is always a good idea to show details of any calculations required as part of your answer.

Check your answer

2. **(a)**

Journal		Dr	Cr	
		$	$	
2017				
Jan 1	Machinery at cost	28 000		(1)
	K Limited		28 000	(1)
	Purchase of machinery on credit			(1)

                                                (3)

Exam tip

Make a point of altering your answer if necessary. This will help you remember the way to answer questions like this and build your confidence in the topic.

(b)

i.

Machinery at cost account									
			$					$	
2016					2016				
Jan	1	K Limited (M1)	24 000	**(1)**	Dec	31	Balance c/d	24 000	
2017					2017				
Jan	1	Balance b/d	24 000		Dec	31	Balance c/d	52 000	
		K Limited (M2)	28 000	**(1)**					
			52 000					52 000	
2018					2018				
Jan	1	Balance b/d	52 000	**(1)**	April	1	Disposal (M1)	24 000	**(1)**
July	1	K Limited (M3)	20 000	**(1)**	Dec	31	Balance c/d	48 000	
			72 000					72 000	
2019									
Jan	1	Balance b/d	48 000	**(1)**					

(6)

ii.

Provision for depreciation of equipment account									
2016			$		2016			$	
Dec	31	Balance c/d	4 800		Dec	31	Income statement (M1)	4 800	**(1)**
2017					2017				
Dec	31	Balance c/d	15 200		Jan	1	Balance b/d	4 800	
					Dec	31	Income statement	10 400	**(1)**
							(M1 $4 800 + M2 $5 600)		
			6 000					6 000	
2018					2018				
April	1	Disposal (M2)	9 600	**(1)**	Jan	1	Balance b/d	15 200	**(1)**
Dec	31	Balance c/d	13 200		Dec	31	Income statement (M2 $5 600 + M3 $2 000)	7 600	**(1)**
			9 000					9 000	
					2019				
					Jan	1	Balance b/d	13 200	**(1)**

Workings (depreciation calculations)

M1: 20% × $24 000 = $4 800

M2: 20% × $28 000 = $5 600

M3: 20% × $20 000 × ½ year = $2 000

(6)

c) Profit or loss on disposal of M1:

	$	
Cost	24 000	**(1)**
Depreciation to date	(9 600)	**(1)**
Net book value at disposal date	14 400	
Sale proceeds	(12 300)	**(1)**
Loss on disposal	2 100	**(1)**

(4)

3. Sundeep's nominal ledger contains the following accounts:

- stationery and office expenses account
- commission received account.

On 1 January 2018 the accounts included the following details:

- stationery and office expenses: office expenses accrued $190
- commission received account: income prepaid $330.

During the year ended 31 December 2018 the Sandeep's cash book recorded the following details:

Receipts:

- commission received $5,420.

Payments:

- stationery $820
- office expenses $2,930.

At 31 December 2018 the following information was available:

- commission accrual $430
- stationery accrual $270
- office expenses prepaid $80.

Prepare the following accounts for the year ended 31 December 2018. Record the transfer to the business's income statement for the year ended 31 December 2018.

(a) stationery and office expenses. **(6)**

(b) commission received. **(4)**

(Total marks: 10)

Common errors

Remember to:

- provide a date (including year) or a narrative placing the credit entry before the debit entry
- provide dates for each entry and record the year on the debit side and credit side of the account each time the year changes
- provide suitable narratives throughout (each purchase should have the narrative K Limited)
- check your calculations of depreciation charges each year, especially in 2018 when the third machine has only been owned for half a year
- provide dates (including years) and suitable narratives
- provide separate transfers for each machine
- correctly label balances – balances must be labelled 'Balance c/d', 'Balance b/d'
- label the final result.

Before you answer the question

Check that you can remember how the opening balances should be recorded, i.e. which are assets (debit balances) and which are liabilities (credit balances).

Remember that care should be taken to record date and narrative details.

Check your answer

3. **(a)**

Stationery and office expenses account							
2018			$	2018			$
Jan-Dec		Bank (stationery)	820 **(1)**	Jan	1	Balance b/d (office expenses)	190 **(1)**
		Bank (office expenses)	2 930 **(1)**	Dec	31	Income statement	3 750 **(1of)**
Dec	31	Balance c/d	270			Balance c/d	80
			4 020				4 020
2019				2019			
Jan	1	Balance b/d (office expenses)	80 **(1)**	Jan	1	Balance (stationery) b/d	270 **(1)**

(6)

(b)

Commission received account							
2018			$	2018			$
Dec	31	Income statement	6 180 **(1of)**	Jan	1	Balance b/d	330 **(1)**
				Jan-Dec		Bank	5 420 **(1)**
				Dec	31	Balance c/d	430
			6 180				6 180
2019							
Jan	1	Balance b/d	430 **(1)**				

(4)

Common errors

Remember to:

- provide accurate narratives (for example, stating 'cheque' or 'payments' instead of 'bank' for the payments)

- bring down the balances on 1 January 2019 (usually marks are only awarded for closing balances if they are brought down)

- record the opening income prepaid balance correctly

- record the closing balance income accrual b/d correctly

- correctly label balances – balances must be labelled 'Balance c/d' and 'Balance b/d'.

Exam tip

Take a few minutes to make notes on your answer. Your notes should include corrections and a brief explanation of what you should have done. You will find that this process will boost your confidence in this topic and prepare you for answering similar questions in the future.

4. On 31 December of its first year, a business's trial balance included trade receivables of $36 000. Based on past experience of irrecoverable debts, it was decided that a provision for doubtful debts should be created at 5 per cent of trade receivables. On 31 December of its second year, trade receivables had increased to $41 000. By 31 December Year 3 trade receivables had decreased to $38 000. The provision for doubtful debts is to be maintained at 5 per cent of trade receivables in years 2 and 3.

(a) Prepare the provision for doubtful debts account for years 1, 2 and 3.

(b) Prepare an extract from the statement of financial position at 31 December, Year 2, showing trade receivables.

Before you answer the question

Look through the details and check whether the provision will be increasing or decreasing in years 2 and 3. This is vital to making the correct entries in answer to **(a)**.

Remember the importance of providing full details in both the ledger account and the extract from the statement of financial position.

Check your answer

4. (a)

Dr				Provision for doubtful debts					Cr
			$						$
Year 2					**Year 1**				
Dec	31	Balance c/d W2	2 050		Dec	31	Income statement W1		1 800
					Year 2				
					Dec	31	Income statement		250
			2 050						2 050
Year 3					Year 3				
Dec	31	Income statement W3	150		Jan	1	Balance b/d		2 050
	31	Balance c/d	1 900						
		W3							
			2 050						2 050
					Year 4				
					Jan	1	Balance b/d		1 900

W1 provision = 5% × $36 000 = $1 800

W2 provision = 5% × $41 000 = $2 050

W3 provision = 5% × $38 000 = $1 900

(b)

Statement of financial position (Extract) at 31 December Year 2			
	$	$	$
CURRENT ASSETS			
Trade receivables	41 000		
Less provision for doubtful debts	2 050		
			38 950

5. Amira's inventory includes some products which have gone out of fashion:

Product	Number of items	Cost per item	Normal selling price per item
S7X	7	$120	$142
T4Z	11	$90	$105

She has decided to have some alterations made to the products which should make them more saleable. The total estimated costs of the alterations for each type of product are:

Product	Cost of alterations
S7X	$180
T4Z	$143

(a) Calculate the total value of the inventory of these products assuming the alterations are made. **(9)**

The following is a summary of a business's results for each of the years ended 31 December 2017 and 31 December 2018:

	for the year ended 31 December:	
	2017	2018
	$	$
Cost of sales	112 000	123 000
Gross profit	82 000	97 000
Profit/(loss) for the year	18 000	(11 000)
Total current assets at year end	45 000	51 000

(b) It has been discovered that the inventory at 31 December 2017 was overvalued by $4 000.

Complete the following table to show revised figures after correcting the overvaluation of inventory: **(8)**

	for the year ended 31 December:	
	2017	2018
	$	$
Cost of sales		
Gross profit		
Profit/(loss) for the year		
Total current assets at year end		

(Total marks: 17)

Before you answer the question

- Remember the importance of showing detailed calculations in the answer to part (a).

- In part (b) remember that one year's closing inventory becomes next year's opening inventory.

Check your answer

5. (a)

Product	Number of items	Cost per item $	Total cost $	Total net realizable value	Valuation $	
S7X	7	120	840 **(1)**	7 × $142 = $994 **(1)** less alterations $180 = $814 **(1)**	814	**(1)**
T4Z	11	90	990 **(1)**	11 × $105 = $1 155 **(1)** less alterations $143 = $1 012 **(1)**	990	**(1)**
				Total value	1 804	**(1)**

(b)

	For the year ended 31 December:	
	2017 $	2018 $
Cost of sales	116 000 **(1)**	119 000 **(1)**
Gross profit	78 000 **(1)**	101 000 **(1)**
Profit/(loss) for the year	14 000 **(1)**	(7 000) **(1)**
Total current assets at year end	41 000 **(1)**	51 000 **(1)**

 Common errors

Remember to:

- show detailed calculations

- use net realizable value (NRV) where it is less than cost and use cost where it is less than NRV

- provide an overall total

- maintain the current assets figure in 2018.

Exam tip

If you made some mistakes, go back and correct them. Make a note of the reasons for any changes required. If you fully understand what went wrong in each case, you will have made real progress in this topic.

Multiple choice questions

1. Which of the following lists contains only revenue expenditure? **(1)**

    A   legal fees paid on purchasing a new retail branch, motor vehicle repair costs, rent of office premises

    B   machinery maintenance charges, buildings insurance, redecoration of the reception area

    C   office salaries, carriage charges on goods for resale, purchase of an office printer

    D   replacement of a worn part on a machine, cost of improving the staff canteen, equipment hire charges

2. Which is a capital receipt? **(1)**

    A   fees received from clients by a firm of accountants

    B   interest received on a bank loan

    C   proceeds from the sale of a non-current asset

    D   rent received for subletting business premises

3. An income statement recorded a draft loss for the year of $2,500. The income statement included carriage inwards of $1,300 paid for the delivery of a non-current asset and a bank loan of $4,300.

    What is the corrected profit or loss for the year? **(1)**

    A   loss $3,100

    B   loss $5,500

    C   profit $500

    D   profit $8,100

4. A business purchased some equipment on 1 January 2016 for $20 000. Depreciation is charged using the reducing-balance method at 20 per cent per annum.

    How much depreciation should be charged for the year ended 31 December 2018? **(1)**

    A $2,560   B $3,200   C $4,000   D $5,000

5. Why is depreciation charged each year on non-current assets? **(1)**

    A   to ensure funds are available to replace the asset

    B   to ensure the accounts show the current market value of the asset

    C   to show when the asset will need replacement

    D   to spread the cost of the asset over its useful life

6. A business owns a motor vehicle which cost $32 000. The vehicle was expected to have a useful life of five years and have a scrap value of $4,000. The vehicle has been depreciated using the straight-line method.

    What is the motor vehicle's net book value at the end of its second year? **(1)**

    A $15 200   B $16 800   C $19 200   D $20 800

7. A business has not yet received interest for the last two months of its financial year.

   How should the closing balance of the interest received account be recorded on the business's statement of financial position? **(1)**

   A current asset, other payables

   B current asset, other receivables

   C current liability, other payables

   D current liability, other receivables

8. A business's rent account had an opening debit balance of $350. During the year the business paid $23 400 for rent. At the year end the accrued rent totalled $420. **(1)**

   What amount for rent should be transferred to the income statement?

   A $22 630   **B** $23 330   **C** $23 470   **D** $24 170

9. A business's financial year ends on 30 November. On 1 August 2018 $900 was paid for insurance for the six months to 28 February 2019.

   What information should be recorded on the business's statement of financial position at 30 November 2018? **(1)**

   A other payable $300   **C** other receivable $300

   B other payable $600   **D** other receivable $600

10. Yasmin has found it necessary to write off the account of trade receivable, HX Retailers, as an irrecoverable debt. What is the double entry for writing off the account? **(1)**

	Debit	Credit
A	HX Retailers	Irrecoverable debts
B	Irrecoverable debts	HX Retailers
C	Irrecoverable debts	Sales
D	Sales	Irrecoverable debts

11. A business maintains a provision for doubtful debts at 5 per cent of trade receivables. At 31 December 2017 trade receivables totalled $10 000; at 31 December 2018 trade receivables totalled $12 000. What will be the effect on the income statement for the year ended 31 December 2018 of the entry for provision for doubtful debts? **(1)**

   A decrease profits $100   **C** increase profits $100

   B decrease profits $600   **D** increase profits $600

12. A business has a provision for doubtful debts of $400. At the end of the current financial year the provision should be changed to $300. What entries are required to change the provision for doubtful debts? **(1)**

	Debit		Credit	
A	Income statement	$100	Provision for doubtful debts	$100
B	Income statement	$300	Provision for doubtful debts	$300
C	Provision for doubtful debts	$100	Income statement	$100
D	Provision for doubtful debts	$300	Income statement	$300

13. Inventories should be valued at the lower of cost or net realizable value. Which accounting principle is being applied? **(1)**

A business entity

B consistency

C prudence

D realization

14. The owner of a business has provided the following details of its closing inventory.

Item	Number of items	Cost price per item	Net realizable value per item
PQ2	100	$7	$5
RB3	200	$6	$8

What is the value of the closing inventory? **(1)**

A $1,700 **B** $1,900 **C** $2,100 **D** $2,300

15. A business's closing inventory has been undervalued.

Which of the following statements correctly states the effect of this error? **(1)**

	Cost of sales	Profit for the year	Current assets
A	overvalued	overvalued	overvalued
B	overvalued	undervalued	undervalued
C	undervalued	overvalued	overvalued
D	undervalued	undervalued	undervalued

(Total marks: 15)

Structured questions

1. Mya owns a wholesale business. Recently the business's warehouse was extended and the following amounts were paid:

	$
Annual insurance premium on warehouse extension	1 000
Carriage charges for materials used in building extension	3 000
Cost of decorating extension	4 000
Cost of installing air conditioning	5 000
Inventory purchased to stock new extension	12 000
Labour costs for building extension	24 000
Material costs for extension	18 000

(a) State what is meant by the term 'capital expenditure'. **(1)**

(b) Calculate the total cost of the warehouse extension. **(6)**

(c) Explain the effect on the calculation of **i.** non-current assets and **ii.** profit for the year, if some items of capital expenditure are treated as revenue expenditure when calculating the cost of the warehouse extension. **(2)**

2. Bakti owns a restaurant. During the year ended 31 December 2018 the following transactions occurred.

Transaction	Revenue expenditure	Capital expenditure	Revenue receipt	Capital receipt
Paid kitchen staff wages				
Sold surplus restaurant furniture				
Purchased additional refrigerators				
Received weekly payments from customers				
Paid for repairs to kitchen equipment				
Took out a bank loan				
Paid carriage charges for the delivery of additional refrigerators				
Discounts received from suppliers of food				
Bakti paid some private funds into the business				
Rent received on sublet premises				

(a) Identify each item as one of: revenue expenditure, capital expenditure, revenue receipt, capital receipt. Place a tick (✔) in the appropriate column. **(10)**

(b) Explain the importance of correctly identifying revenue expenditure and capital expenditure. **(3)**

3. Carla owns Maxi Retail Stores. The shop's fixtures and fittings were purchased on 1 January 2017 for $18 500. Carla has provided depreciation each year on the fixtures and fittings to take account of wear and tear.

(a) State **three** causes of depreciation of non-current assets other than wear and tear. **(3)**

(b) Carla's accounting year ended on 31 December. She provides depreciation on non-current assets using the reducing-balance method at 20 per cent per annum.

Prepare the provision for depreciation of fixtures and fittings account for each of the years ended 31 December 2017 and 2018. **(5)**

(c) Prepare an extract from the business's statement of financial position at 31 December 2018 showing fixtures and fittings. **(3)**

4. Vikash owns a business providing taxis in a busy city centre.

At 31 December 2017, the accounting year end, the business owned the following taxis:

Taxi 1	Cost $30 000	Purchased 1 January 2015
Taxi 2	Cost $33 000	Purchased 1 January 2016
Taxi 3	Cost $35 000	Purchased 1 October 2017

Vikash's policy is to depreciate taxis by 20 per cent per annum using the straight-line method. Depreciation is provided in the year of purchase on a month-by-month basis, but no depreciation is provided in the year of sale.

(a) Prepare a journal entry to record the depreciation of taxi 1 on 31 December 2015. A narrative is required. **(3)**

(b) Prepare an extract from the trial balance at 31 December 2016 recording details of the business's taxis. **(3)**

(c) Calculate the total provision for depreciation on taxis for the year ended 31 December 2017. **(4)**

(d) Taxi 1 was sold on 14 August 2018 for $12 800.

Prepare the journal entries required to record the disposal of taxi 1. Narratives are not required. **(6)**

(e) Prepare the disposal account for taxi 1 in the business's nominal ledger. **(4)**

5. A business's nominal ledger included the following accounts:

- insurance
- rent receivable
- motor vehicle repairs

At 1 October 2017 rent receivable was prepaid $380 and motor vehicle repairs $320 was accrued.

During the year the business's cash book included the following details:

2017–2018		$	2017–2018		$
Oct- Sept	Rent receivable	3 940	Oct-Sept	Insurance	3 960
				Motor vehicle repairs	1 840

The following information was available at 30 September 2018:

- The amount paid during the year for insurance includes a premium of $570 which provided cover for the business for the three months ended 30 November 2018.

- The tenant had not paid rent of $350 per month for the three months ended 31 October 2018.

(a) Explain how the matching principle is applied to the calculation of a business's profit. **(2)**

(b) Prepare the following accounts for the year ended 30 September 2018:

i. insurance **(3)**

ii. rent receivable **(4)**

iii. motor vehicle repairs. **(3)**

6. A business's nominal ledger includes one expense account for oil and electricity. The business's financial year ends on 31 August.

On 1 September 2017 oil supplies had been prepaid $920 and there was an amount owing for electricity of $480.

During the year ended 31 August 2018 payments were made for oil $3,290 and for electricity $1,370.

The owner of the business uses part of the business premises for private use. It is estimated that $640 of oil and electricity charges relates to this part of the premises.

At 31 August 2018, oil supplies were accrued $530 and electricity charges had been prepaid $270.

(a) Prepare the heat and light account for the year ended 31 August 2018. **(8)**

(b) State how the balances of the oil and electricity account should appear on the business's statement of financial position at 31 August 2018. **(2)**

7. On 1 February 2018, Seema sold goods on credit to PX Ltd for $1,420. On 1 July 2018 Seema was made aware that PX Ltd would not be able to pay the amount due. On 4 July 2018 Seema was advised to apply the principle of prudence and write off the amount owing from PX Ltd.

(a) Define the term 'irrecoverable debt'. **(1)**

(b) Explain how writing off an irrecoverable debt is an application of the principle of prudence. **(2)**

(c) Prepare a journal entry in Seema's books to record writing off the irrecoverable debt. **(3)**

(d) On 11 December 2018 Seema received a cheque from PX Ltd for $1,420 in payment of the debt which had been written off on 4 July 2018.

Prepare the account of PX Ltd showing all the entries required in 2018. **(4)**

8. Shilpa owns A1 Computer Services. Her business provides support for local businesses experiencing problems with computer technology. On 31 July 2018 she extracted the following list of balances from her books of account:

	$
Debts recovered	550
Discounts allowed	210
Insurance	3 950
Irrecoverable debts written off	620
Office expenses	4 990
Motor vehicles	
cost	37 400
provision for depreciation 1 August 2017	11 200
Provision for doubtful debts 1 August 2017	560
Rent of premises	10 200
Revenue	118 930
Staff wages	63 580
Trade receivables	17 800

The following additional information was available at 31 July 2018:

- Insurance prepaid amounted to $280.

- Staff wages owing amounted to $1,840.

- Motor vehicles should be depreciated by 25 per cent, per annum using the reducing-balance method.

- The provision for doubtful debts should be maintained at 5 per cent of trade receivables.

(a) Explain why Shilpa should maintain a provision for doubtful debts account. **(3)**

(b) Prepare the provision for doubtful debts account for the year ended 31 July 2018. **(3)**

(c) Prepare an income statement for the year ended 31 July 2018. **(14)**

9. The owner of a business has been valuing the closing inventory.

(a) State **two** reasons for ensuring closing inventory is not overvalued. **(2)**

(b) Explain what is meant by the term 'net realizable value'. **(2)**

(c) The business has the following unsold items at the 31 December 2018:

Item	Number of items	Cost per item $	Normal selling price per item $	Total estimated costs to ensure items are in a saleable condition $
H3B	12	11	16	65
J2C	20	14	20	73
K7D	8	23	31	41
L5E	14	8	13	78
M6F	7	4	8	30

Prepare a statement of inventory valuation at 31 December 2018 to show the correct total valuation of inventory at this date. **(16)**

(d) Calculate by how much the business's profit for the year would have been overvalued if all the items had been valued at cost. **(2)**

(Total marks: 127)

Unit 5:
Preparation of financial statements

Unit outline

All financial statements are based on the same fundamental principles, but their presentation and content will vary depending on the form of ownership and type of business. Financial statements are prepared for service, trading and manufacturing businesses and ownership can take the form of a sole trader, a partnership or a limited liability company. Clubs and societies also prepare financial statements.

This unit provides details of how to prepare financial statements for all these forms of organization.

Either tick these boxes to build a record of your revision, or use them to identify your strengths and weaknesses.

Your revision checklist

Specification	Theme	☺	☺	☹
5.1 Sole traders	5.1.1 Sole trader background			
	5.1.2 Statements of financial position			
	5.1.3 Adjustments and the income statement			
5.2 Partnerships	5.2.1 Advantages and disadvantages of forming a partnership			
	5.2.2 Partnership agreements			
	5.2.3 Financial statements			
	5.2.4 Format for partners' ledger accounts and financial statements			
5.3 Limited companies	5.3.1 The background to limited companies			
	5.3.2 The financial statements of a limited company			
5.4 Clubs and societies	5.4.1 Receipts and payments accounts and income and expenditure accounts			
	5.4.2 Revenue-generating activities			
	5.4.3 Income and expenditure account format			
5.5 Manufacturing accounts	5.5.1 Direct and indirect costs, factory overheads and prime cost			
	5.5.2 Work in progress; calculating cost of production			
	5.5.3 Preparing the annual financial statements of a manufacturing organization			
	5.5.4 Adjustments to financial statements			
5.6 Incomplete records	5.6.1 Disadvantages of not keeping a full set of accounting records			
	5.6.2 Preparing income statements and statements of financial position from incomplete information			
	5.6.3 Using ratios to find missing information			

You will need to know how to:

- explain the advantages and disadvantages of operating as a sole trader
- explain the importance of preparing income statements and statements of financial position
- prepare income statements for trading businesses and service businesses
- explain that statements of financial position record assets and liabilities on a specific date
- recognize and define the content of a statement of financial position
- prepare statements of financial position for trading and service businesses
- make adjustments for provisions for depreciation using straight-line, reducing-balance and revaluation methods
- make adjustments for accrued and prepaid expenses and accrued and prepaid income
- make adjustments for irrecoverable debts, provisions for doubtful debts and goods taken by the owner for personal use.

5.1.1 Sole trader background

Advantages and disadvantages of operating as a sole trader

Advantages	Disadvantages
• Sole traders have complete control over the operation of the business	• Decision making may be impaired if the sole trader has limited understanding of key aspects of running a business
• Decision making is faster as there is no one else to consult	• Sole traders have **unlimited liability** for the debts of their businesses
• All profits belong to the sole trader	
• A sole trader business is comparatively easy to set up and may require only a small amount of capital	• A sole trader may find it difficult to take time away from running the business
• There is no legal requirement to publish financial statements	• It may be difficult to raise additional finance to expand a business

The importance of the financial statements

A sole trader's financial statements provide the most important source of information for the owner when assessing the performance of the business.

- The income statement provides details about the business's gross profit (if it is a trading business) and profit or loss for the year.

- The statement of financial position provides details of the business's resources.

The owner's assessment will lead to key decisions about the business's future, for example:

- how to improve profits
- whether to invest in additional resources
- how to raise finance to make improvements.

The format for income statements

A trading business sells goods for a profit and as a result its income statement includes details of goods bought and sold having taken account of changes in inventory during the financial period as well as the business's general running costs.

A service business, however, earns its income through providing a service to its customers or clients. No goods are involved, so its income statement is more straightfoward.

> **Exam tip**
>
> There is more about how financial statements are assessed in Unit 6.

Trading business	Service business

Trading business

Name of business

Income statement for the year ended (date in full)

	$	$
Revenue	xxx	
Less returns inwards	(xxx)	
		xxx
Less: cost of sales		
Opening inventory	xxx	
Purchases	xxx	
Less returns outwards	(xxx)	
Carriage inwards	xxx	
	xxx	
Closing inventory	(xxx)	
		(xxx)
Gross profit		xxx
Add: other income		xxx
		xxx
Less: expenses	xxx	
expenses	xxx	
		(xxx)
Profit for the year		xxx

Service business

Name of business

Income statement for the year ended (date in full)

	$	$
Revenue/fees		xxx
Add: other income		xxx
		xxx
Less: expenses	xxx	
expenses	xxx	
		(xxx)
Profit for the year		xxx

Notes:

- The statement begins with the income from the service provided – this could be in the form of fees.
- Add any other income before listing and deducting all the business's running costs.

Notes:

- It is important to label key figures: cost of sales, gross profit and profit for the year.
- In the cost of sales section, record items in the order shown.
- The income statement is made up of two sections: the trading section and the profit and loss section.

It is important to remember that income statements are formal documents, so they require high standards of presentation. For example:

- always include the name of the business (if known)
- the title should be written in full without abbreviations
- place negative figures in brackets
- if the business makes a loss, the final result will be labelled 'loss for the year', and the amount will be shown in brackets.

An income statement can be presented in horizontal form, with costs debited to the statement and income credited to the statement. The vertical form of presentation is preferred as it a more accessible format for non-specialists.

Recap

1. Sole traders enjoy several advantages, of which being in complete control of a business is often the most rewarding.

2. Sole traders also suffer from several disadvantages, chief of which is unlimited liability.

3. The income statements of trading and service statements differ in that the former includes a trading section showing details of revenue less cost of sales, whereas the latter includes a single section showing income less expenses.

Apply

1. Ravi is a trader. During the year ended 31 December 2018 his business had revenue of $300 000. The cost of sales was made up of: opening inventory $27 000, purchases $188 000, returns outwards $17 000, carriage inwards $3,000, closing inventory $24 000.

   (a) Calculate the business's cost of sales.

   (b) Calculate the business's gross profit.

2. Serena owns a financial services agency. During the year ended 31 December 2018 she received fees from clients of $147 000 and the business's expenses were $118 000. Calculate the business's profit for the year.

Review

There are more details about the sole traders, income statements and service businesses in section 5.1 of *Essential Accounting for Cambridge IGCSE® & O Level (third edition)*, pages 208–9.

5.1.2 Statements of financial position

A statement of financial position sets out a business's resources (assets) and how these resources have been financed (liabilities and capital/owner's equity) at a specific date.

Format of a statement of financial position

Name of business Statement of financial position at (year)			
	$	$	$
Assets			
Non-current assets	Cost	Accumulated depreciation	Net
Goodwill	xxx		xxx
Property	xxx	xxx	xxx
Motor vehicles	xxx	xxx	xxx
Equipment	xxx	xxx	xxx
	xxx	xxx	xxx
Current assets			
Inventory		xxx	
Trade receivables	xxx		
Less provision for doubtful debts	(xxx)		
		xxx	
Other receivables		xxx	
Cash at bank		xxx	
Cash in hand		xxx	
			xxx
Total assets			xxx
Capital and liabilities			
Capital			
Opening balance		xxx	
Add profit for year		xxx	
		xxx	
Less drawings		(xxx)	
			xxx
Non-current liabilities			
Bank loan			xxx
Current liabilities			
Trade payables		xxx	
Other payables		xxx	
Total capital and liabilities			xxx

Presentation is important. The title should include the name of the business and the title in full without abbreviations. Each section should be subtotalled. Negative figures (the provision for doubtful debts, drawings and a loss for the year) should be shown in brackets.

The format for a statement of financial position is almost identical for a trading and service business, except in the latter case there will be no inventory to record as a service business does not hold goods for resale.

Goodwill is an **intangible asset** and it is shown first in the list of a business's non-current assets. Other receivables include prepaid expenses and income accruals. In the capital section a loss for the year should be deducted from the opening capital figure. Other payables include accrued expenses and prepaid income.

The current liabilities section could include an overdraft bank balance. The items shown in a statement of financial position are linked by the accounting equation (see Unit 1). One important consequence is that the totals of a statement of financial statement should agree; if they do not agree, then an error (or errors) must have been made.

Assets and liabilities are usually listed in order of permanence. The most permanent (long-lasting) items are shown first and the least permanent (most frequently changing) items are shown last. The order of items can be reversed and shown in order of liquidity.

A statement of financial position could be presented in a horizontal format with assets shown on the left-hand side and capital and liabilities shown on the right-hand side. However, the vertical form of presentation is preferred.

Recap

1. A statement of financial position sets out the detail of a business's resources and how they are financed on a specific date.

2. Each section of the statement (non-current assets, current assets, capital, non-current liabilities and current liabilities) should have a subheading and a subtotal.

Apply

3. A business has the following details to be recorded on its statement of financial position at a particular date:

   i. other receivables

   ii. petty cash

   iii. bank loan repayable in three months' time

   iv. loss for the year.

   For each item, state in which section it should be recorded.

Review

There are more details about statements of financial position in section 5.2 of *Essential Accounting for Cambridge IGCSE® & O Level (third edition)*, pages 210–12.

> **Exam tip**
>
> It is a common mistake to include a bank loan repayable in just a few months' time (i.e. less than a year) in the non-current liabilities section instead of the current liabilities section.

5.1.3 Adjustments and the income statement

Details within an income statement will be affected by various adjustments.

Example with adjustments shown in italics

Asif Market Traders
Income statement for the year ended 31 December 2018

	$	$
Revenue	193 000	
Less returns inwards	(1 800)	
		191 200
Less: cost of sales		
Opening inventory	11 700	
Purchases	93 500	
Less returns outwards	(800)	
Less goods own use	*(200)*	
Carriage inwards	600	
	104 800	
Closing inventory	(10 100)	
		(94 700)
Gross profit		96 500
Add: *profit on disposal of equipment*	*100*	
Decrease in provision for doubtful debts	*200*	
Interest receivable (received $550 + $50 accrued income)	*600*	
Rent receivable (received $3 800 – $300 prepaid income)	*3 500*	
		4 400
		100 900
Less: expenses		
General expenses (paid $16 700 + $300 accrued expense)	*17 000*	
Insurance (paid $2 300 – $200 prepaid expense)	*2 100*	
Irrecoverable debts written off	*500*	
Loss on disposal of motor vehicle	*800*	
Depreciation charges		
Equipment ($18 000 cost × 20%, straight-line method)	*3 600*	
Motor vehicles ($38 000 nbv × 25%, reducing-balance method)	*9 500*	
		(33 500)
Profit for the year		**67 400**

An income statement could show an increase in the provision doubtful debts which should appear in the list of expenses. An income statement could show depreciation of non-current assets based on the valuation method.

⏱ **Review**

There are more details about the sole traders, income statements and service businesses in section 5.1 of *Essential Accounting for Cambridge IGCSE® & O Level (third edition)*, pages 208–9.

Exam tip

Where adjustments are made to items in an income statement, it is strongly recommended that detailed workings are provided to show how the final figures were derived.

For more details on how adjustments are made, see sections 4.1–4.5.

⏪ **Recap**

1. A wide range of adjustments may be made to items in an income statement.

2. Goods for own use should be deducted from purchases in an income statement.

✏ **Apply**

4. State how the following adjustments will affect the calculation of a business's profit for the year – increase or decrease.

   (a) A motor vehicle with a net book value of $7,300 was sold for $7,100.

   (b) The provision for doubtful debts was increased.

   (c) The owner took goods for own use.

   (d) Income was prepaid.

   (e) There were accrued expenses.

You will need to know:

- the advantages and disadvantages of forming a partnership
- the importance and contents of a partnership agreement
- the purpose of an appropriation account
- how to prepare income statements, appropriation accounts and statements of financial position
- how to record interest on partners' loans, interest on capital, interest on drawings, partners' salaries and the division of the balance of profit or loss
- how to make adjustments to financial statements
- how to draw up partners' capital and current accounts in ledger account form and as part of a statement of financial position.

5.2.1 Advantages and disadvantages of forming a partnership

Advantages	Disadvantages
A partnership may be able to raise more capital than a sole trader	Profits are shared between the partners
Each partner can contribute expertise and skills to benefit the business	Each partner has unlimited liability for the debts of the business
It is easier to manage the business as the workload can be shared	Decision making can take longer as each partner's agreement is required for key decisions
Decision making can be better informed because each partner can contribute to the discussion	Each partner is jointly responsible for the debts of the business (even if a partner was not directly involved in incurring the debt)
Losses are shared by all the partners	Partnerships can be short lived, as the death or retirement or a partner could close the business
	There is a chance of disagreement, which can impact the success of the business

Recap

Partnerships enjoy important advantages – most notably the possibility of having more capital and shared expertise. However, there can be difficulties, particularly the question of whether the partners will get along.

Apply

1. Two successful sole traders are considering entering into partnership. Explain why this may not necessarily be a good idea.

2. Define the term 'unlimited liability'.

Review

For full details about why individuals form partnerships, see section 5.3 of *Essential Accounting for Cambridge IGCSE® & O Level (third edition)*, page 217.

5.2.2 Partnership agreements

Partners are advised to make an agreement to avoid disputes which can lead to the closure of the business. If a formal written document is prepared this is referred to as a **deed of partnership**.

Partners can include the following in an agreement:

- capital contributions (often fixed)
- how profits and losses will be divided (this could be as simple as equal shares, or could be in the form of a ratio)
- limits on drawings per annum
- the responsibilities of each partner for the management of the business
- the rate of interest to be provided on any loan made by a partner
- whether partners are to be penalized by charging **interest on drawings** when sharing profits
- whether partners are to be rewarded before sharing profits by providing **interest on capital** contributions or a **partnership salary** for undertaking some particular role in managing the partnership.

◀◀ Recap

1. Formal agreements between partners will help minimize serious disagreements.
2. Agreements can include quite elaborate arrangements for sharing profits and losses.
3. Agreements can also clarify management responsibilities.

✎ Apply

3. Identify some of the risks which could arise if partners do not make an agreement.
4. Contrast a partnership salary with an employee's salary.

⏱ Review

For more information about partnership agreements and the sharing of profits and losses, see sections 5.4 and 5.5 of *Essential Accounting for Cambridge IGCSE® & O Level (third edition)*, pages 218–21.

5.2.3 Financial statements

A partnership's income statement will closely resemble that of a sole trader. It will need to take account of all the adjustments described in Unit 4. Interest on a partner's loan should be included in the income statement.

An **appropriation account** shows in detail how profits or losses for the year are to be shared between each partner. Interest on drawings is added to the profit for the year, whereas interest on capital and partnership salaries is deducted.

A statement of financial position resembles that of a sole trader for the following sections:

• non-current assets

• current assets

• current liabilities.

Non-current liabilities could include loans from partners. The capital section is set out to show details of each partner's capital contributions and separate information from each partner's **current account**.

 Common errors

Don't forget that end-of-year financial statements must always be presented with full headings. Avoid using any abbreviations in the titles of financial statements.

 Recap

1. End-of-year financial statements are prepared in the same way as those of a sole trader, but also include an appropriation account to show how profits and losses are to be shared between the partners.

 Apply

5. Explain why interest on drawings and interest on capital are treated differently in an appropriation account.

 Review

For more about partnership financial statements, see section 5.7 of *Essential Accounting for Cambridge IGCSE® & O Level (third edition)*, pages 224–5.

5.2.4 Format for partners' ledger accounts and financial statements

Appropriation account

Appropriation account for the year ended 31 December 2018		
	$	$
Profit for the year		xxx
Add: interest on drawings		
Y	xxx	
Z	xxx	
		xxx
		xxx
Less: salary (Y)		(xxx)
		xxx
Less: interest on capitals		
Y	xxx	
Z	xxx	
		(xxx)
		xxx
Less: shares of remaining profit		
Y	xxx	
Z	xxx	
		(xxx)

The profit (or loss) for the year is transferred from the income statement. It is recommended that interest on drawings is recorded next and added to the profit for the year; then each share of profit (salary, interest on capital, etc.). It is recommended that subtotals are shown after each appropriation.

Fixed capital accounts

A **fixed capital account** records the agreed and unchanging capital contribution of a partner.

Dr			Capital accounts			Cr
	Y	Z		Y	Z	
	$	$		$	$	
			Balance b/d	xxx	xxx	

Only if all the partners agree should additional entries be made in the capital account for any withdrawal of capital (debit entry) or any addition to capital (credit entry).

⊗ Common errors

One common mistake is to deduct interest on drawings rather than add it to the profit for the year.

Exam tip

Don't forget that interest on a partner's loan is an expense to be recorded in the income statement.

Current accounts

Dr			Current accounts		Cr
	Y	Z		Y	Z
	$	$		$	$
Opening balance b/d			Opening balance b/d	xxx	xxx
Drawings	xxx	xxx	Salary	xxx	
Interest on drawings	xxx	xxx	Interest on capital	xxx	xxx
Balance c/d		xxx	Interest on loan		xxx
			Share of profit	xxx	xxx
			Balance c/d	xxx	
	xxx	xxx		xxx	xxx
Balance b/d	xxx		Balance b/d		xxx

Current accounts are used to record the day-to-day changes in a partner's investment in the business.

During the year, drawings are recorded in a separate account, and the balance of the account is transferred to the partner's current account at the year end.

A partner's current account can have a debit balance (indicating that a partner's drawings have exceeded shares of profit) or a credit balance (indicating that a partner's shares of profit have exceeded drawings). A debit balance implies the partner is in debt to the partnership; a credit balance implies the partnership is in debt to the partner.

All increases are credited to the current account (including any interest on a loan transferred from the income statement).

All decreases are debited to the current account (including any share of a loss).

Statement of financial position

Summarized version

Statement of financial position (Extract) at 31 December 2018			
	Y	Z	
	$	$	$
Capital accounts	xxx	xxx	xxx
Current accounts	(xxx)	xxx	xxx
			xxx

Detailed version

Statement of financial position (Extract) at 31 December 2018			
	Y	Z	
	$	$	$
Capital accounts	xxx	xxx	xxx
Current accounts			
Opening balance	xxx	xxx	
Salary	xxx		
Interest on loan	xxx	xxx	
Shares of profit	xxx	xxx	
	xxx	xxx	
Drawings	(xxx)	(xxx)	
Interest on drawings	(xxx)	(xxx)	
	xxx	xxx	xxx
			xxx

The statement of financial position resembles that of a sole trader, except that the non-current liabilities could include details of loans from partners, and the capital section will require details about each partner.

The capital section can be set out showing just the final balances of the capital and current accounts. Alternatively, the current accounts can be set out in detail.

Where partners have fixed capital, it is important that subtotals for capital accounts and current accounts are shown separately. Negative figures should be shown in brackets.

Apply

6. Jamal is in partnership with Ayesha. During the year ending 31 December 2018 the partnership made a small profit of $26 000. The partnership agreement provides for a salary for Jamal of $8,000 per annum after charging interest on drawings at 10 per cent on total drawings for the year. Remaining profits or losses are shared equally. Over the year, Jamal's drawings totalled $24 000 and Ayesha's drawings totalled $30 000. The balance on Jamal's current account on 1 January 2018 was $1,300 credit.

(a) Calculate Jamal's share of the profit for the year.

(b) Prepare Jamal's current account for the year.

Review

For illustrations of partnership financial records, see sections 5.6 and 5.7 of *Essential Accounting for Cambridge IGCSE® & O Level (third edition)*, page 222–5.

Recap

1. In most partnerships, partners choose to have fixed capital which cannot be altered without the agreement of all the partners.

2. Day-to-day changes in a partner's investment are recorded in drawings accounts and current accounts (which include the transfer of total drawings for the year).

3. The statement of financial position at the financial year end must show details of each partner's fixed capital and either just the current account balance at that date or full details of each partner's current accounts, as well as the final balance.

You will need to know how to:

- explain the advantages and disadvantages of operating as a limited company
- explain the meaning of the terms 'limited liability' and 'equity'
- explain the capital structure of a limited company comprising preference share capital, ordinary share capital, general reserve and retained earnings
- explain and distinguish between share capital and loan capital
- prepare income statements, statements of changes in equity and statements of financial position
- make adjustments to financial statements.

5.3.1 The background to limited companies

Advantages and disadvantages of operating as a limited company

Advantages	Disadvantages
Shareholders have **limited liability** for the debts of the company. Shareholders can only lose what they have agreed to invest in the company.	Companies are subject to more regulation than sole traders and partnerships.
A company has a separate legal identity. Any legal action is taken against the company; shareholders are not held personally responsible.	Companies must publish annual financial statements, so details of performance can be accessed by anyone.
Companies can access more sources of finance than sole traders and partnerships.	Costs arise from the additional regulation.
It is easier to transfer ownership (shares) so companies enjoy continuity of existence.	

Features of limited companies

Ownership	Shareholders are the owners of a limited company who receive a dividend as their share of the profits of the company.
Directors	Directors are individuals responsible for running and managing a limited company. They are appointed by the shareholders and report annually to them. Directors may also be shareholders in the company.
Public limited company (plc)	This is a type of limited company which may offer its shares to members of the public. Shares can be traded on recognized stock exchanges.
Private limited company (Ltd)	This is a type of limited company which cannot offer its shares to the general public. Usually the shareholders are members of a family and sometimes friends of the family.
Ordinary shares	These are the most common type of share; sometimes called **equity** shares. Each share carries one vote, so the more shares owned by an individual shareholder the greater the degree of control which can be exercised at the company's annual general meeting. Dividends paid on ordinary shares vary as they are dependent on the profit made by the company and the directors' views about what the company can afford. If a company is liquidated, ordinary shareholders are the last to have their investment repaid. Therefore, ordinary shareholders are the main risk-takers.
Preference shares	Preference shareholders receive a fixed rate of dividends and receive their dividends ahead of ordinary shareholders. They take preference over ordinary shareholders in the event of a company being liquidated. Preference shareholders do not have voting rights. Preference shares can be redeemable (i.e. repayable), in which case they are treated as a non-current liability rather than part of the company's capital. If preference shares are non-redeemable (i.e. a permanent investment) they form part of the company's capital structure.
Reserves	Reserves are profits which have not been distributed to shareholders. Undistributed profits are referred to as retained earnings. Directors may transfer some of a company's retained earnings to a general reserve to indicate to shareholders that it is unlikely this amount will be distributed as dividends in the near future.
Equity	This is the term used for the total funds provided by the shareholders of a company. It is made up of issued shares plus undistributed profits.

Dividends	The rewards paid to shareholders from a company's profits are called dividends. Where there are available profits dividends are usually paid annually.
	The directors may also pay an interim (mid-year) dividend. Dividends can only be provided if there are profits available and cash with which to pay the dividends. Dividends paid are recorded in the statement of changes in equity. Dividends proposed by directors but not yet paid are not recorded in the financial statements (they appear as a note in the published accounts). Dividends paid on redeemable preference shares are recorded in the income statement instead of the statements of changes in equity, as these shares are regarded as a non-current liability.
Authorized capital	This is the maximum amount of shares which may be issued by a company. The figure is agreed when the company is established.
Issued capital	This is the amount of share capital which has actually been issued by a company. The figure will either be equal to the authorized capital or less than the authorized capital.
Called-up capital	Directors may decide to issue shares with payment being made in instalments in accordance with an agreed timescale. Called-up share capital is the amount requested by the directors at any point in time.
Paid-up share capital	This is the amount which shareholders have actually paid towards the called-up share capital.
Debentures	These are a form of finance and are long-term loans repayable at a stated future date. Debentures have a fixed rate of interest. Debenture interest must be paid each year whether or not a company is making a profit. Debenture interest is shown as a finance cost in a company's income statement. If a company is liquidated, debenture holders are repaid before shareholders. Debentures are recorded as non-current liabilities on a company's statement of financial position. Debentures are shown with certain details on a statement of financial position.

Recap

1. There are two main types of limited company: public and private.

2. Ownership is by means of shares.

3. There are two main types of share: ordinary and preference.

4. The reward for shareholders is the payment of a dividend financed by the profits of the company.

5. Undistributed profits are called reserves and there are two main types: retained earnings and general reserve.

6. Equity is the term used for the total of share capital and reserves.

7. Only a proportion of the amount due might have been asked for and this is referred to as the called-up capital.

8. The amount actually received from a share issued is referred to as the paid-up capital.

9. Limited companies can raise further finance through long-term loans called debentures.

Review

There is more about the background to limited companies in sections 5.8–5.10 in *Essential Accounting for Cambridge IGCSE® & O Level (third edition)*, pages 231–6.

Apply

1. A limited company has issued share capital of 300 000 ordinary shares of $1 each. The shareholders are required to pay 50 per cent of the amount due immediately, 25 per cent one year later and the remaining sum after two years. One investor has purchased 84 000 shares. Calculate:

   (a) the total called-up capital after 18 months

   (b) the amount the investor pays immediately the shares are issued.

2. A company has issued 700 000 shares at $0.50 each and 100 000 6 per cent non-redeemable preference shares of $1 each. One investor has purchased 220 000 ordinary shares and 20 000 preference shares. Calculate:

   (a) the total issued share capital of the company

   (b) the amount invested in ordinary shares by the investor

   (c) the preference share dividend to be paid to the investor each year if the company makes sufficient profits.

3. A company's statement of financial position includes the following: 8 per cent debentures (2027) $360 000. State:

   (a) what is meant by (2027)

   (b) the annual interest to be paid on the debentures.

5.3.2 The financial statements of a limited company

Income statement format

Income statement for the year ended (date)	
	$
Revenue	xxx
Cost of sales	(xxx)
Gross profit	xxx
Administrative expenses	(xxx)
Distribution expenses	(xxx)
Profit from operations	xxx
Finance costs	(xxx)
Profit for the year	xxx

Limited company income statements are based on the same principles as those for the income statements of sole traders and partnerships (i.e. matching, prudence and consistency).

Many companies now prepare their income statements in summarized form, as shown in the table above. For example, cost of sales can be shown without the detail of inventories or purchases. Alternatively, the income statement could be set out showing fuller details about cost of sales and expenses.

Expenses are grouped together under three headings:

- administration

- distribution

- finance.

Finance costs include debenture interest, loan interest and the dividend paid on redeemable preference shares.

An important feature is that a subtotal is shown before deducting finance costs, i.e. profit from operations.

Statement of changes in equity format

This statement details the changes during a financial year in each element in a company's equity.

Statement of changes in equity for the year ended (date)					
	Ordinary share capital	Preference share capital	General reserve	Retained earnings	Total
	$	$	$	$	$
Balances (date at beginning of year)	xxx	xxx	xxx	xxx	xxx
Profit for year				xxx	xxx
Dividends paid				(xxx)	(xxx)
Transfer to general reserve			xxx	(xxx)	---
Balances (date at end of year)	xxx	xxx	xxx	xxx	xxx

Common errors

- Remember to label the subtotals: gross profit, profit from operations, profit for the year.

Dividends should only include amounts actually paid during the year. This could include interim dividends and final dividends on ordinary shares and non-redeemable preference shares.

Statement of financial position

A limited company's statement of financial position closely resembles that of a sole trader and partnership. The main differences occur in recording the equity and non-current liabilities sections:

Statement of financial position at (date)			
	$	$	$
Assets	Cost	Accumulated depreciation	Net
Non-current assets	xxx	(xxx)	(xxx)
Current assets			
Inventory		xxx	
Trade receivables		xxx	
Other receivables		xxx	
Bank		xxx	
			xxx
Total assets			xxx
EQUITY			
Shares and reserves			
Issued share capital			
Ordinary shares of $1 each		xxx	
6% preference shares of $1 each		xxx	
General reserve		xxx	
Retained earnings		xxx	
Total equity			xxx
Non-current liabilities			
8% debentures (2025)			xxx
Current liabilities			
Trade payables		xxx	
Other payables		xxx	
			xxx
Total equity and liabilities			xxx

 Common errors

Some students fail to provide a full description for each entry in the statement. Sometimes students fail to realize that a transfer to the general reserve results in a nil entry in the total column.

In a statement of financial position, ordinary shares are recorded before non-redeemable preference shares in the equity section, and a general reserve is recorded before retained earnings.

The capital section is headed 'equity', and consists of issued share capital plus reserves. The detail shown in this section will correspond to the final totals shown in the statement of changes in equity.

It is good practice to record the labels: 'total assets', 'total equity' and 'total equity and liabilities'.

◀◀ Recap

1. Limited companies' financial statements are based on the usual accounting principles.

2. The income statement has some differences from that of a sole trader or partnership. An additional subtotal, called profit from operations, is shown after deducting administrative and distribution expenses from gross profit.

3. Profit for the year is found by deducting finance costs (e.g. interest on debentures) from profit from operations.

4. Limited companies prepare a statement of changes in equity to show how share capital and reserves have changed from the beginning of the year to the end of the year.

5. The main difference when preparing a statement of financial position is that the capital section is headed 'equity' and that it records issued capital and details about reserves.

✏ Apply

4. A limited company has made a gross profit of $180 000. Administrative expenses total $29 000, distribution costs are $37 000 and finance costs are $9,000. Calculate:

   (a) the profit from operations

   (b) the profit for the year.

5. On 1 January 2018 a limited company had retained earnings of $80 000. During the year it made a profit of $135 000. The directors paid a dividend of $0.20 per share on the issued capital of 500 000 ordinary shares of $1 and made a transfer of $40 000 to the general reserve. Calculate retained earnings at 31 December 2018.

⏱ Review

There are detailed illustrations of the financial statements of limited companies in sections 5.11–5.13 in *Essential Accounting for Cambridge IGCSE® & O Level (third edition)*, pages 237–41.

- distinguish between receipts and payments accounts and income and expenditure accounts
- prepare receipts and payments accounts
- prepare accounts for revenue-generating activities
- prepare income and expenditure accounts and statements of financial position
- make adjustments to financial statements
- define and calculate the accumulated fund.

5.4.1 Receipts and payments accounts and income and expenditure accounts

Receipts and payments account	Income and expenditure account
A summary of a cash book	Similar to a business's income statement
Designed to show members what has caused the club's cash resources to change over a year	Designed to show whether the club's income for a year is sufficient to cover its expenditure
Includes all cash and bank transactions	Based on the matching (accruals) principle
Both accounts will help club officials decide whether the club is financially viable or whether action needs to be taken to increase cash resources and improve the club's income.	

Preparing a receipts and payments account

Name of club Receipts and payments account for the year ended (date)			
Receipts		**Payments**	
	$		$
Opening balance (cash and bank balances) b/d	xxx	Expenses	xxx
Members' subscriptions	xxx	Purchases of non-current assets	xxx
Donations	xxx	Closing balance (cash and bank balances) c/d	xxx
Receipts from activities	xxx		
Proceeds from the sale of non-current assets	xxx		
	xxx		xxx
Balance b/d	xxx		

The receipt and payments account summarizes all cash and bank transactions, including all amounts received during the year (revenue and capital receipts) as well as all amounts paid (revenue and capital expenditure).

The opening balance and/or the closing balance could be overdrawn, and therefore shown as a credit balance.

Recap

1. A **receipts and payments account** is a summary of the cash book maintained by the treasurer of a club.

2. An **income and expenditure account** is similar to a business's income statement.

3. Both statements are designed to help the club's membership understand the financial position of the club.

Apply

1. A treasurer reports that the club had an opening balance of cash at the bank of $3,560, total receipts of $14 920 and total payments of $16 230. What was the club's closing balance of cash at the bank?

2. A club's receipts and payments account is being prepared. The following details are to be entered in the account:

    i.   opening bank balance (overdrawn) – $1,230

    ii. subscriptions received from members – $18 450

    iii. ticket sales for social events – $3,580

    iv. running expenses paid – $8,430

    v.   purchase of additional equipment – $5,200

    vi. costs of social events – $2,560.

    What was the club's closing bank balance?

Review

There is a detailed illustration of a receipts and payments account in section 5.14 of *Essential Accounting for Cambridge IGCSE® & O Level (third edition)*, on pages 247–9.

5.4.2 Revenue-generating activities

Members' subscriptions

Most clubs depend on members' subscriptions as their major source of revenue.

The receipts and payments account shows the amount actually received during the year.

The income and expenditure account must comply with the matching (accruals) concept and show the amount which should have been received during the year. This means making adjustments for any subscriptions due and unpaid and for any subscriptions received in advance.

Calculating subscription income			
Adjustments at the YEAR END			
Subscriptions due but not yet received		Subscriptions received in advance	
	$		$
Receipts during the year	xxx	Receipts during the year	xxx
Add subscription due at the year end	xxx	*Less* subscriptions received in advance at the year end	(xxx)
Income for the year	xxx	Income for the year	xxx

Calculating subscription income			
Adjustments at the BEGINNING OF THE YEAR			
Subscriptions due but not yet received		Subscriptions received in advance	
	$		$
Receipts during the year	xxx	Receipts during the year	xxx
Less subscriptions due at beginning of the year	(xxx)	*Add* subscriptions received in advance at beginning of the year	xxx
Income for the year	xxx	Income for the year	xxx

Summarizing the matching concept: amounts relating to the year under review should be included; amounts relating to the previous year or to the next year should be excluded.

Account format for subscriptions

Subscriptions account			
	$		$
Opening balance (subscriptions due for the previous year) b/d	xxx	Opening balance (subscriptions received in advance for the current year) b/d	xxx
Income for the current year (transferred to the income and expenditure account)	xxx	Receipts during the year	xxx
Closing balance (subscriptions received in advance for the next year) c/d	xxx	Closing balance (subscriptions due for the current year) c/d	xxx
	xxx		xxx
Balance b/d (subscriptions due)	xxx	Balance b/d (subscriptions received in advance)	xxx

Fundraising and trading activities

A club may raise funds by organizing activities designed to make a profit. The success of these activities needs to be clearly shown in the income and expenditure account.

Where the information is straightforward the details can be shown within the income and expenditure account – it is important the net result of the activity is clearly indicated.

Where the information is more complicated the details should be shown in a separate account.

- A trading account should be used if it is a trading activity, such as a café, with the profit or loss on the activity transferred to the income and expenditure account.

- A profit and loss account should be used for a non-trading activity, such as a social evening or sports competition – again the net result of the activity must be transferred to the income and expenditure account.

Recap

1. The main source of income for most clubs is from members' subscriptions.

2. All subscriptions received during a year are entered in the receipts and payments account.

3. In accordance with the matching (accruals) principle, only subscription income for a year is entered in the income and expenditure account. As a result, adjustments have to be made for subscriptions due and subscriptions received in advance.

4. Clubs can also try to increase their income by providing activities designed to make a profit.

5. If the information about a revenue-raising activity is complex, a separate account should be prepared to show the profit (or loss).

6. The profit or loss made on each revenue-raising activity should be recorded in the income and expenditure account.

Apply

3. A club has 430 members. The annual membership subscription is $25 per member. During 2018 subscriptions for that year were received from 405 members. Eighteen members also paid their subscription for 2019. Calculate:

   (a) the club's subscription income for 2018

   (b) the amounts received from members for subscriptions during 2018.

4. On 1 January 2018, a club was owed $560 by members for subscriptions for 2017. During the year, subscriptions received totalled $23 400. This sum included the subscriptions owing for 2017 and subscriptions of $920 received in advance for 2019. Subscriptions due for 2018 but unpaid totalled $600. Calculate the club's subscription income for 2018.

5. A club provides refreshments for its members. On 1 January 2018 the club had an inventory of unsold refreshments valued at $450. During 2018, the club paid refreshments suppliers $14 320 and refreshment sales totalled $19 230. At 31 December 2018 the inventory of unsold refreshments was valued at $880 and $1,050 was owing to refreshment suppliers. Calculate the profit on refreshments for 2018.

 ### Review

There is more about revenue-raising activities in section 5.16 of *Essential Accounting for Cambridge IGCSE® & O Level (third edition)*, pages 252–4.

5.4.3 Income and expenditure account format

Name of club Income and expenditure account for the year ended (date)			
	$	$	$
INCOME			
Members' subscriptions		xxx	
Profit on café		xxx	
Sports competition			
Sales of tickets	xxx		
Less competition prizes	(xxx)		
		xxx	
Donations		xxx	
Profit on disposal of non-current asset		xxx	
			xxx
EXPENDITURE			
Expenses		xxx	
Depreciation of non-current assets			
Loss on social evening			
Sales of tickets	xxx		
Less expenses	(xxx)		
		xxx	
Loss on disposal of non-current asset		xxx	
			xxx
Surplus for year			xxx

If the club's expenditure is more than its income, the result will be recorded as 'Deficit for year' rather than 'Surplus for year', and the figure will appear in brackets.

All revenues and expenses must be adjusted in accordance with the matching (accruals) principle.

Statement of financial position; the accumulated fund

The format will closely resemble that of a business, with subheadings for non-current assets, current assets and current liabilities.

The accumulated fund replaces the capital section. It should consist of an opening balance (the value of the club at the beginning of the year) plus the surplus for the year (or less the deficit for the year). It should end with a subtotal representing the value of the club at the end of the year.

The **accumulated fund** is in effect a total of the accumulated surpluses made by a club over a period of years.

The opening balance of the accumulated fund may have to be calculated. This can be done using the accounting equation, i.e. listing and totalling assets at the beginning of the year, and listing and deducting liabilities at the end of the year.

Particular care is needed when recording subscriptions due (which are an asset) and subscriptions received in advance (which are a liability).

Recap

1. The matching (accruals) principle is applied when preparing a club's income and expenditure account.

2. The term 'surplus' is used instead of profit, and 'deficit' is used instead of loss.

3. A club's statement of financial position records the club's non-current assets, current assets and liabilities.

4. As a club does not have any owners, the subheading 'accumulated fund' is used instead of capital. The accumulated fund is the net total of all the club's surpluses over its existence.

Apply

6. Which items from the following list should be included in an income and expenditure account?

   i. depreciation of non-current assets

   ii. receipts from social events

   iii. purchase of new equipment

   iv. loss on refreshments

   v. loan repayments

   vi. donations from members

   vii. loss on sale of unwanted furniture.

7. On 31 December 2018 a club had non-current assets valued at $83 400, subscriptions of $1,200 due, subscriptions of $1,420 received in advance, a bank overdraft of $3,200 and clubhouse rent prepaid at $440. What was the club's accumulated fund on this date?

Review

There are illustrations of income and expenditure accounts and statements of financial position in sections 5.15 and 5.17 in *Essential Accounting for Cambridge IGCSE® & O Level (third edition)*, pages 250–1 and 255–6.

You will need to know how to:

- distinguish between direct and indirect costs
- explain the terms 'direct material', 'direct labour', 'prime cost' and 'factory overhead'
- explain and make adjustments for work in progress
- calculate factory cost of production
- prepare manufacturing accounts, income statements and statements of financial position
- make adjustments to financial statements.

5.5.1 Direct and indirect costs, factory overheads and prime cost

Direct costs	
Explanation	A cost which can be linked to making one product. It will be known just how much of each **direct cost** is required to make one product.
Examples	• Direct materials (the raw materials used to make the product) • Direct labour (the cost of labour actually making a product, operating machinery, assembling the product, etc.)
Treatment	Direct costs are added together to find the **prime cost**.

Indirect factory costs	
Explanation	A cost which cannot be linked to making one product. It will be impossible to know just how much of an **indirect cost** is required to make one product.
Examples	• Factory rent • Factory maintenance costs • Factory lighting and heating • Depreciation of factory non-current assets (machinery, factory buildings, etc.) • Indirect labour costs (factory manager's salary, factory supervisors' salaries, wages of maintenance staff, wages of factory cleaners, etc.) • Indirect material costs (cost of machine-lubricating oil, factory cleaning materials, etc.)
Treatment	Indirect factory costs are added together to find a total for **factory overheads**.

◀◀ **Recap**

1. In a manufacturing organization, costs are divided into two categories: direct and indirect.

2. Direct costs can be linked to making one product.

3. Indirect costs cannot be linked to making one product.

4. The distinction is important when preparing a manufacturing account which is designed to find the total cost of production for a year.

Apply

1. A manufacturing business buys several types of materials for use in its factory. Describe how you decide whether the materials should be regarded as a direct cost or an indirect cost.

2. Give two examples of different types of labour costs which should be regarded as indirect labour in a manufacturing business.

Review

There is more information about direct and indirect costs in sections 5.18 and 5.19 of *Essential Accounting for Cambridge IGCSE® & O Level (third edition)*, pages 263–4.

5.5.2 Work in progress; calculating cost of production

At the end of a financial period it is almost certain that there will be items in the production line which are unfinished. These partly completed goods are called **work in progress**.

The **manufacturing account** is designed to find the total cost of producing all completed goods, so the value of any work in progress at the year end is excluded.

Goods which were only partly finished at the end of one year will be finished in the next year, so their value (the opening inventory of work in progress) is added to the cost of production in the next year.

Cost of production is calculated as follows:

Direct cost + Indirect cost + Opening inventory of work in progress-closing inventory of work in progress

Recap

1. When preparing a manufacturing account, it is necessary to take account of the value of any partly finished goods.

2. An adjustment is made for both opening and closing inventories of work in progress.

Apply

3. In its first year of manufacture, a business spent $100 000 on direct costs and $80 000 on indirect costs. There was a closing inventory of work in progress valued at $10 000. What was the cost of production of finished goods in Year 1?

4. In its second year the business spent $140 000 on direct costs and $95 000 on indirect costs. As well as the opening value of work in progress there was a closing inventory of work in progress valued at $15 000. What was the cost of production of finished goods in Year 2?

Review

There is an illustration of a manufacturing account including work in progress in section 5.20 of *Essential Accounting for Cambridge IGCSE® & O Level (third edition)*, pages 266–7.

5.5.3 Preparing the annual financial statements of a manufacturing organization

Format: manufacturing account

Manufacturing account for the year ended (date)			
	$	$	$
Raw materials			
Opening materials		xxx	
Purchases	xxx		
Less returns outwards	(xxx)		
	xxx		
Add carriage inwards	xxx		
		xxx	
		xxx	
Less closing inventory		(xxx)	
Cost of raw materials consumed			xxx
Direct labour			xxx
Prime cost			xxx
Factory overheads		xxx	
Factory expenses		xxx	
Indirect labour		xxx	
Indirect materials		xxx	
Depreciation of factory non-current assets		xxx	
			xxx
			xxx
Adjustment for work in progress			
Add opening inventory		xxx	
Less closing inventory		(xxx)	
			xxx
Cost of production			xxx

It is important to provide the three labels for key figures in the manufacturing account (shown in bold in the table on the previous page).

In effect, the manufacturing account is an addition of all the costs associated with making the product – including any factory expenses.

The net figure for the adjustment for work in progress could be negative if the closing inventory is more than the opening inventory.

Format: income statement

Income statement for the year ended (date)		
	$	$
Revenue	xxx	
Less returns inwards	(xxx)	
		xxx
Opening inventory of finished goods	xxx	
Add cost of production	xxx	
Purchases of finished goods	xxx	
	xxx	
Less closing inventory of finished goods	(xxx)	
Cost of sales of finished goods		(xxx)
Gross profit		xxx
Add other income		xxx
		xxx
Less expenses:		
Administration expenses	xxx	
Distribution expenses	xxx	
Financial costs	xxx	
Selling expenses	xxx	
Depreciation of non-factory non-current assets	xxx	
		(xxx)
Profit for the year		xxx

The three labels shown in bold in the example above should always be shown.

The trading section of the income statement is concerned only with finished goods.

Sometimes a manufacturer will feel it necessary to buy in finished goods from another manufacturer. For example, this could occur if the manufacturer has a contract to supply goods, but for some reason (e.g. machine breakdown) too few items have been produced.

The expenses shown in an income statement must not include any relating to the factory.

Format: statement of financial position

Statement of financial position (Extract) at (date)			
	$	$	$
CURRENT ASSETS			
Inventories			
Raw materials		xxx	
Work in progress		xxx	
Finished goods		xxx	
			xxx

The three inventories should be shown in detail in the statement of financial position. A subtotal of the three inventories should also be included.

 Common errors

- Remember: the trading section is for finished goods only.
- Don't include factory expenses in the income statement.
- Remember to label the three key items: cost of sales, gross profit, profit for the year.

◀◀ Recap

1. The financial statements of a manufacturing organization include:

   - a manufacturing account designed to find the total cost of finished goods (the cost of production)

   - an income statement which shows the gross profit and net profit (or loss) for the year

   - a statement of financial position which closely resembles that of other types of business.

2. Adjustments for prepaid expenses, accruals, depreciation, provisions for doubtful debts, etc. are likely to affect financial statements.

✏️ Apply

5. At the end of a financial year, a manufacturer provided the following details concerning direct materials:

   i. opening inventory – $41 000

   ii. purchases – $823 000

   iii. returns outwards – $7,000

   iv. carriage inwards – $4,000

   v. closing inventory – $44 000.

   What was the manufacturer's cost of raw materials consumed?

Apply

6. During a financial year a manufacturing company had:

    i. raw materials consumed – $327 500

    ii. direct wages – $402 600

    iii. depreciation of factory non-current assets – $72 000

    iv. indirect materials – $5,700

    v. indirect labour costs – $31 800

    vi. other factory running costs – $81 000

    vii. an adjustment for work in progress – $11 400 (positive).

    What was the manufacturer's prime cost and cost of production?

7. A manufacturer had a cost of production of $600 000, an opening inventory of finished goods $17 800, a closing inventory of finished goods $19 400, purchases of finished goods $8,500 and revenue $973 000. What was the manufacturer's gross profit?

Review

See section 5.20 for an illustration of the financial statements of a manufacturing organization in *Essential Accounting for Cambridge IGCSE® & O Level (third edition)*, pages 266–8.

5.5.4 Adjustments to financial statements

A manufacturer's financial statements may require all the adjustments which affect the financial statements of retail, wholesale and service businesses in line with the matching (accruals) and prudence concepts. These include:

- expense accruals and prepayments

- income due and received in advance

- depreciation of non-current assets

- provisions for doubtful debts.

It may be necessary to show the allocation of certain expenses between the factory (to be shown in the manufacturing account) and the office in the income statement; and sometimes to divide certain expenses between direct costs and indirect costs in the manufacturing account.

For example, if one rent account is maintained it will be necessary to divide the rent for the year between the factory and the office in an appropriate ratio based on floor area.

Recap

1. All the usual adjustments could apply to a manufacturer's financial statements.

2. Some expenses may need to be divided between the manufacturing account and the income statement, or between direct and indirect costs.

Apply

8. A manufacturer paid rent of $39 400 during a financial year. At the end of the year, rent of $1,600 had been prepaid. Rent is divided between the factory and the office in the ratio 3:1. The manufacturer also paid $525 000 in wages: 70 per cent of this figure was for machine operatives, 10 per cent was for factory supervisors, and 20 per cent was for office staff.

9. State how rent and wages should be recorded in the manufacturer's financial statements.

Review

The illustration in section 5.20 of *Essential Accounting for Cambridge IGCSE® & O Level (third edition)*, pages 266–8 includes adjustments.

- explain the disadvantages of not maintaining a full set of accounting records
- prepare opening and closing statements of affairs
- calculate profit or loss for the year from changes in capital over time
- calculate sales, purchases, gross profit, trade receivables and trade payables and other figures from incomplete information
- prepare and make adjustments to income statements and prepare statements of financial position from incomplete information
- apply the techniques of mark-up, margin and inventory turnover to arrive at missing figures.

5.6.1 Disadvantages of not keeping a full set of accounting records

Where details records of transactions are not maintained the following problems can arise.

- There is limited or no access detailed information about aspects of the business.
- Financial statements are difficult to prepare.
- The performance of the business cannot be assessed.
- Decision making to improve performance will be hampered because analysis of current weaknesses is limited or non-existent.
- Information is not available to support loan applications.
- Reliable information for tax assessments may not be available.

Calculating profits from changes in capital over time

Where there is very limited information the technique used to calculate profits, losses is as follows:

Step 1	Calculate the business's capital at the beginning of the year under review. This means assembling details about assets and liabilities on this date and preparing a **statement of affairs**. Using the accounting equation will enable the opening capital to be determined $(A = C + L)$
Step 2	Calculate the business's capital at the end of the year under review. Prepare a second statement of affairs at this date to find the closing capital.
Step 3	Assemble information about the owner's drawings and any capital contributions during the year under review.
Step 4	Combine the details about opening capital, drawings, capital contributions and closing capital to find the profit (or loss) for the year. (See the format for this calculation below.)

Calculating profit or loss in the form of a statement

	$	$
Closing capital	xxx	80 000
Less opening capital	(xxx)	(60 000)
Subtotal (increase or decrease in capital during the year)	xxx	20 000
Deduct additions to capital (as these should not be included in the profit for the year)	(xxx)	(5 000)
Add back drawings (to arrive at the figure for profit before the drawings took place)	xxx	18 000
Profit (or loss) for the year	xxx	33 000

Calculating profit or loss in the form of a capital account

In the capital account below, the dates are given as an example:

Dr			Capital account					Cr
2018			**$**	**2018**				**$**
Jan–Dec		Drawings	18 000	Jan	1	Balance b/d		60 000
Dec	31	Balance c/d	80 000	June	12	Bank		5 000
				Dec	31	Profit for year		33 000
			98 000					98 000
				2019				
				Jan	1	Balance b/d		80 000

◀◀ **Recap**

1. Sole traders who choose not to keep full accounting records can experience difficulties in managing their business effectively.

2. Without a full accounting system there is often insufficient information to make informed decisions.

3. Where there is minimal information it is possible to calculate a business's profits by reconstructing a capital account where profit is the one missing item of information.

4. A business's capital can be calculated by constructing a statement of affairs which lists assets and liabilities at a particular date.

✏️ **Apply**

1. The following information is available about a business:

    i. capital at the beginning of the year – $112 000

    ii. capital at the year end – $124 000

    iii. drawings during the year –$27 500

    iv. additional capital invested by the owner during the year – $6,000.

   Calculate the business's profit or loss for the year.

2. A business started trading on 1 January 2018 with capital of $92 000. During the year the owner withdrew cash $17 000 and goods $1,500 for own use. The owner also made an additional investment in the business of $7,500 in June 2018. At 31 December 2018 the business had assets of $101 000 and liabilities of $23 000. Calculate the business's profit or loss for 2018.

 **Review**

There is more about statements of affairs and calculating profit and losses from minimal information in sections 5.21 and 5.22 in *Essential Accounting for Cambridge IGCSE® & O Level (third edition)*, pages 275–7.

5.6.2 Preparing income statements and statements of financial position from incomplete information

In the absence of ledger accounts, the following techniques can be used to find the figures required for the preparation of financial statements. These techniques can be used where there are records of opening and closing balances, and receipts and payments (for example on bank statements).

Credit sales

Credit sales are calculated by reconstructing a total trade receivables account. In its simplest form this means including the:

- total of opening balances of trade receivables
- total of receipts from trade receivables
- total of closing balances of trade receivables.

But all transactions affecting trade receivables should be included, so additional entries should be made for discounts allowed.

Credit purchases

A similar process is used to find credit purchases requiring the preparation of a total payables account which will include the:

- total of opening balances of trade payables
- total of payments to trade payables
- total of closing balances of trade payables.

The total payables account could also include discounts received.

Total sales and total purchases

Total sales = credit sales + cash sales

Total purchases = credit purchases + cash purchases

Expenses and income

Expenses for inclusion in the income statement
= Payments made during the year
+ Amounts due but unpaid at the year end
– Amounts prepaid at the year end

Income or inclusion in income statement
= Receipts during the year
+ Amounts due but not yet received
– Amounts received in advance

Common errors

Where discounts allowed and received are included in the calculations, it is easy to forget that these items must be included in the income statement as well.

Closing bank and cash balances

When preparing a cash account and/or bank account:

Opening balance + receipts – payments = closing balance

Missing cash

If you are asked to identify missing cash, prepare a cash account and include all the known information. The missing figure will be a credit entry. The missing cash could be for drawings (but the question will clarify this).

Recap

1. There are a variety of techniques which can be used to calculate the figures required to prepare an income statement in situations where a business does not have full accounting records.

2. By preparing total trade payables accounts and total trade receivables accounts it is possible to find credit purchases and credit sales as the missing figures.

3. It may be necessary to adjust payments for expenses for accruals and prepayments at both the beginning and end of the year.

4. It may be necessary to adjust receipts for income for amounts due and amounts received in advance at both the beginning and end of the year.

✏️ Apply

3. The following details are available about a business:

   i. opening balance of trade payables – $17 400

   ii. closing balance of trade payables – $22 900

   iii. payments to trade payables – $248 300

   iv. discounts received – $2,400.

   Calculate the business's purchases.

4. The owner of a business has supplied the following information about trade receivables for a year:

   i. opening balance – $11 900

   ii. closing balance – $8,300

   iii. receipts – $141 900

   iv. discounts allowed – $2,100.

   Calculate the business's credit sales.

5. A business rents its premises. The following information is available about a financial year:

   i. opening balance rent due but unpaid – $1,450

   ii. payments during the year – $14 900

   iii. closing balance rent prepaid – $850.

   Calculate the business's rent expense for the year.

6. A business receives interest on some investments. At the beginning of a financial year interest of $450 was due, interest received during the year was $5,220 and interest due but not yet received at the year end was $620. Calculate the business's income from interest for the year.

⏱ Review

There is more about the techniques used to find missing information in section 5.23 of *Essential Accounting for Cambridge IGCSE® & O Level (third edition),* pages 278–80.

5.6.3 Using ratios to find missing information

The following ratios can be used to find missing information in the trading section of an income statement, such as a closing inventory, purchases or revenue.

Ratio	Formula
Mark-up percentage	*Cost of sales × 100/revenue*
Gross margin	*Gross profit × 100/revenue*
Rate of inventory turnover	*Cost of sales /average inventory*

It can be useful to be able to convert mark-up to gross margin and vice versa. in certain situations. The following table gives two examples of how to do this.

Converting mark-up to gross margin		Converting gross margin to mark-up	
Assume mark-up is 25% (i.e. ¼)		Assume gross margin is 33⅓% (i.e. ⅓)	
Assemble a skeleton trading section to show the ratio details in a simple form			
Revenue	?	Revenue	3
Cost of sales	4	Cost of sales	?
Gross profit	1	Gross profit	1
Complete the missing element in the trading section			
Revenue	❺	Revenue	3
Cost of sales	4	Cost of sales	❷
Gross profit	1	Gross profit	1
The gross margin is ⅕, i.e. 20%		The mark-up is ½, i.e. 50%	

◀◀ Recap

1. Missing details in the trading section of an income statement can sometimes be found by using accounting ratios.

2. Gross margin, mark-up and rate of inventory turnover are the ratios which can be used.

3. Sometimes it will be necessary to convert mark-up to gross margin, and vice versa.

✎ Apply

7. A business's revenue during a financial year was $250 000. The business always applies a gross margin of 20 per cent. Calculate the business's cost of sales.

8. A business's revenue during financial year was $660 000. The business always applies a mark-up of 25 per cent. Calculate the business's gross margin as a percentage and its cost of sales.

9. A business's revenue during a financial year was $450 000. The business always applies a gross margin of 50 per cent. The business had an opening inventory of $23 500 and a rate of inventory turnover of ten times for the year under review. Calculate the business's closing inventory.

⏱ Review

There are more details about the use of ratios to find missing figures and a full illustration of incomplete records in sections 5.24 and 5.25 of *Essential Accounting for Cambridge IGCSE® & O Level (third edition)*, pages 281–5.

Exam-style questions

1. Amhan owns Palmbeach Stores. His business' financial year ended on 31 December 2018 when the following information was available:

Trial balance at 31 December 2018		
	$	$
Bank loan (repayable 31 March 2019)		4 500
Bank loan interest	410	
Bank overdraft		740
Carriage inwards	1 220	
Cash in hand	360	
Capital		133 900
Drawings	19 930	
Furniture and equipment		
cost	12 300	
provision for depreciation		4 920
General expenses	11 270	
Insurance	3 110	
Inventory 1 January 2018	15 430	
Irrecoverable debt	620	
Loss on disposal of equipment	180	
Motor vehicles		
cost	27 800	
provision for depreciation 1 January 2018		15 400
Premises		
cost	145 000	
provision for depreciation		10 500
Provision for doubtful debts		410
Purchases	125 420	
Rent receivable		4 980
Returns outwards		1 390
Revenue		227 600
Trade payables		11 230
Trade receivables	14 200	
Wages	38 320	
	415 570	415 570

Additional information:

- At 31 December 2018 inventory was valued at $15 300.

- Rent receivable $340 was prepaid at 31 December 2018.

- Amhan took goods valued at $480 for own use during the year. This had not been recorded in the books of account.

- Insurance $480 had been paid to cover the business for the three months ending 31 January 2019.

- Wages $1,850 were accrued at 31 December 2018.

- Amhan's policy is to depreciate non-current assets as follows:

  - furniture and equipment – 20 per cent per annum using the straight-line method

  - motor vehicles – 25 per cent per annum using the reducing-balance method

  - premises - $3,500 per annum.

- The provision for doubtful debts should be increased by $70.

(a) Prepare the income statement for the year ended 31 December 2018.   **(18)**

(b) Prepare the statement of financial position at 31 December 2018.   **(11)**

(Total marks: 29)

Before you answer the question

There is a lot to do in this question, so it is important to spend a few minutes looking through the trial balance to identify those items which will be recorded in the income statement and those which will be entered in the statement of financial position. You might wish to make a note beside each item about how it should be treated.

Study the additional information carefully. You could make a note beside the items which need adjustment. Keep in mind the importance of presenting your answer well (without abbreviations) and providing workings.

Check your answer

1. (a)

Palmbeach Stores

Income statement for the year ended 31 December 2018

	$	$	$	
Revenue			227 600	
Less: cost of sales				
Opening inventory		15 430		**(1)**
Purchases	125 420			**(1)**
Less returns outwards	(1 390)			**(1)**
Less goods for own use	(480)			**(1)**
Carriage inwards	1 220			**(1)**
		124 770		
		140 200		
Less closing inventory		(15 300)		**(1)**
			(124 900)	**(1)**
Gross profit			102 700	**(1)**
Add: rent receivable ($4 980 **(1)** – $340)			4 640	**(1)**
			107 340	
Less expenses				
Bank loan interest		410		
General expenses		11 270		**(1)**
Insurance [$3 110 **(1)** – (⅓ × $480)]		2 950		**(1)**
Irrecoverable debt		620		
Loss on disposal of equipment		180		**(1)**
Increase in provision for doubtful debts		70		**(1)**
Wages ($38 320 + $1 850)		40 170		
Depreciation of non-current assets				
Furniture and equipment ($12 300 × 20%)		2 460		**(1)**
Motor vehicles [25% × ($27 800 - $15 400)]		3 100		**(1)**
Premises		3 500		
			(64 730)	
Profit for the year			42 610	**(1)**

(18)

(b)

Statement of financial position at 31 December 2018				
Assets	$	$	$	
Non-current assets	Cost	Accumulated depreciation	Net	
Premises	145 000	14 000	131 000	**(1)**
Motor vehicles	27 800	18 500	9 300	**(1)**
Furniture and equipment	12 300	7 380	4 920	**(1)**
	185 100	39 880	145 220	
Current assets				
Inventory		15 300		
Trade receivables	14 200			**(1)**
Less provision for doubtful debts	(480)			**(1)**
		13 720		**(1)**
Other receivables		160		**(1)**
Cash in hand		360		
			29 540	
Total assets			174 760	
Capital and liabilities				
Capital				
Opening balance		133 900		
Add profit for the year		42 610		**(1)**
		176 510		
Less drawings ($19 930 + $480)		(20 410)		**(1)**
			156 100	
Current liabilities				
Bank loan		4 500		**(1)**
Trade payables		11 230		
Other payables ($340 + $1 850)		2 190		**(1)**
Bank overdraft		740		
			18 660	
Total capital and liabilities			174 760	

(11)

2. Annie and Ryan are in a partnership, sharing profits and losses in the ratio 3:2. Their partnership agreement provides for: interest on total drawings of 5 per cent, interest on capital at 10 per cent per annum and a partnership salary of $8,000 per annum for Annie.

   (a) Describe two possible disadvantages of being in partnership rather than operating as a sole trader. **(2)**

   (b) State one reason why Annie may have made a loan to the partnership rather than increasing her capital contribution. **(1)**

⊗ Common errors

Remember to:

- provide proper headings for each statement and avoid the use of any abbreviations (e.g. Dec for December)

- include labels for cost of sales, gross profit, profit for the year

- include details of calculations arising from the adjustments (workings could be shown within the income statement or provided separately)

- deduct the figure for goods taken for own use from purchases

- provide subheadings and subtotals in **(b)**

- record the bank loan as a current liability

- provide full details of trade receivables: the closing balance, the amended provision for doubtful debts and the final net figure.

Remember that:

- the prepaid insurance was for one month rather than for three months.

The following details have been taken from the partnership books at 31 December 2018 after the gross profit for the year had been calculated:

	$	
Administration expenses	9 940	
Capital accounts		
Annie	60 000	
Ryan	50 000	
Current accounts, 1 January 2018		
Annie	820	credit
Ryan	3 250	debit
Drawings		
Annie	18 800	
Ryan	21 400	
Gross profit for year	64 200	
Loan from Annie	7 500	
Profit on disposal of equipment	620	
Wages and salaries	42 690	

Additional information:

- 'Administration expenses' includes a payment of $3,600 which covers the three-month period ending 28 February 2019.

- Annie is entitled to receive interest of 8 per cent per annum on her loan. No interest was paid during 2018. The balance of the loan account remained unchanged throughout 2018.

- Depreciation of $5,600 should be provided on furniture and equipment.

(c) Prepare the second section of the income statement for the year ended 31 December 2018. **(6)**

(d) Prepare an appropriation account for the year ended 31 December 2018. **(9)**

(e) Prepare Annie's current account for the year ended 31 December 2018. Balance the account on 31 December 2018. **(7)**

(Total marks: 25)

Before you answer the question

Look through all the information and think about where each item will be recorded in your answer.

Work out how the additional information will affect the answer. Workings should always be shown for more complex calculations.

Keep in mind the importance of presenting financial statement well – avoiding abbreviations in the titles of financial statements, for example.

Check your answer

2. (a) Two from:

- profits are shared between the partners **(1)**

- decision making can take longer as each partner's agreement is required for key decisions **(1)**

- each partner is jointly responsible for the debts of the business (even if a partner was not directly involved in incurring the debt) **(1)**
- chance of disagreements which could impact on the success of the business. **(1)**

(1 mark each; maximum 2 marks)

(b) One from:

- the partnership only requires a temporary increase in finance
- Annie will require these funds later for her personal use
- Annie has spare funds and the interest rate offered on the loan is attractive. **(1)**

(c)

Annie and Ryan			
Income statement for the year ended 31 December 2018			
		$	$
Gross profit			64 200
Add: profit on disposal of equipment			620 **(1)**
			64 820
Less: expenses			
Administration expenses $9 940 (1) – *prepaid* $2 400 (⅔ × $3 600)		7 540 **(1)**	
Loan interest (Annie) (8% × $7 500)		600 **(1)**	
Wages and salaries		42 690	
Depreciation of furniture and equipment		5 600	**}(1)**
			56 430
Profit for year			8 390 **(1)**

(d)

Appropriation account for the year ended 31 December 2018			
Profit for the year			8 390 **(1)**
Add: interest on drawings			
Annie (5% × $18 800)		940 **(1)**	
Ryan (5% × $21 400)		1 070 **(1)**	
			2 010
			10 400 **(1)**
Less: interest on capital			
Annie (10% × $60 000)		6 000 **(1)**	
Ryan (10% × $50 000)		5 000 **(1)**	
			11 000
			(600) **(1)**
Less: salary for Annie			8 000 **(1)**
			(8 600)
Less: shares of remaining loss			
Annie		5 160	
Ryan		3 440 **(1)**	
			8 600

(e)

Dr		Current account – Annie							Cr	
			$						$	
2018					2018					
Dec	31	Drawings	18 800	**(1)**	Jan	1	Balance b/d		820	
	31	Interest on drawings	940	**(1)**	Dec	31	Interest on capital		6 000	**(1)**
	31	Share of loss	5 160	**(1)**		31	Salary		8 000	**(1)**
						31	Interest on loan		600	**(1)**
						31	Balance c/d		9 480	
			24 900						24 900	
2019										
Jan	1	Balance b/d	9 480	**(1)**						

Common errors

- Task **(c)**:
  - miscalculating the adjustment in administration expenses: the prepayment is for just two months, not three months
  - failing to include Annie's loan interest in the income statement, but recording it in the appropriation account instead
  - not always labelling items correctly – failing to label 'profit for the year', or stating 'depreciation' rather than 'depreciation of furniture and equipment', for example.
- Task **(d)**:
  - subtracting rather than adding interest on drawings
  - incorrect calculation of the share of loss based on the agreed profit/loss sharing ratio.
- Task **(e)**:
  - not including dates (which should also include the year)
  - confusion over which side to record entries, i.e. debit side for decreases, credit side for increases
  - failing to balance the account and carry the balance down.

Exam tip

Spend a little time correcting your mistakes.

In tasks **(a)** and **(b)** cross out any incorrect points and add any point(s) you overlooked.

In tasks **(c)**, **(d)** and **(e)** write in corrections when you have worked out why your answer was wrong.

Remember: time spent understanding why your answer is incorrect will ensure you improve your performance.

3. W Ltd have an issued share capital of 800 000 ordinary shares of $1 each, fully paid. On 1 January 2018 the company's retained earnings were $84 000 and there was a general reserve of $60 000. The following details are available for the year ending 31 December 2018:

	$
Administrative expenses paid	48 000
Cost of sales	325 000
8% debentures (2024)	100 000
Debenture interest paid	4 000
Distribution expenses paid	37 000
Dividends paid	80 000
Revenue	580 000

Additional information at 31 December 2018:

- Administration expenses of $6,000 were prepaid.

- Distribution expenses of $4,000 were accrued.

- Debenture interest for the half year ended 31 December 2018 has not yet been paid.

- The directors have decided to transfer $30 000 to the general reserve.

(a) Prepare the income statement for the year ended 31 December 2018. **(11)**

(b) Prepare the statement of changes of equity for the year ended 31 December 2018. **(5)**

(c) Prepare an extract from the statement of financial position at 31 December 2018, showing the company's equity. **(4)**

(Total marks: 20)

Before you answer the question

Look through the information carefully and make decisions about how to treat each item and which of the three statements required in the answer will be affected.

Remember the importance of good presentation: use full headings and label the subtotals correctly.

Check your answer

3. (a)

W Ltd		
Income statement		
for the year ended 31 December 2018		
	$	
Revenue	580 000	**(1)**
Cost of sales	(325 000)	**(1)**
Gross profit	255 000	**(1)**
Administrative expenses ($48 000 **(1)** - $6 000)	(42 000)	**(1)**
Distribution expenses ($37 000 **(1)** + $4 000)	(41 000)	**(1)**
Profit from operations	172 000	**(1)**
Finance costs (8% × $100 000) **(1)**	(8 000)	**(1)**
Profit for the year	164 000	**(1)**

(11)

(b)

Statement of changes in equity at 31 December 2018					
	Ordinary share capital	General reserve	Retained earnings	Total	
	$	$	$	$	
Balances 1 January 2018	800 000	60 000	84 000	944 000	(1)
Profit for year			164 000	164 000	(1)
Dividends paid			(80 000)	(80 000)	(1)
Transfer to general reserve		30 000	(30 000)	–	(1)
Balances at 31 December 2018	800 000	90 000	138 000	1 028 000	(1)

(c)

Statement of financial position at 31 December 2018 (Extract)			
	$	$	
EQUITY			
Shares and reserves			
Issued share capital			
Ordinary shares of $1 each	800 000		(1)
General reserve	90 000		(1)
Retained earnings	138 000		(1)
Total equity		1 028 000	(1)

4. The following information for the year ended 31 December 2018 is available for the Valeford Sports Club:

Receipts and payments account for the year ended 31 December 2018			
Receipts		**Payments**	
	$		$
Opening bank balance b/d	636	Suppliers of café refreshments	1 392
Members' subscriptions	8 420	Wages of grounds staff	2 835
Donations	800	Wages of café staff	643
Café sales	2 289	Sports competition prizes	1 272
Sports competition receipts	1 145	Rent of clubhouse and sports grounds	2 200
		Purchase of new sports equipment	3 500
		Closing bank balance c/d	1 448
	13 290		13 290
Balance b/d	1 448		

	1 January 2018	31 December 2018
	$	$
Inventory (café refreshments)	890	970
Subscriptions due	–	340
Subscriptions received in advance	280	160
Rent of clubhouse and grounds prepaid	–	180
Wages of grounds staff due	–	120
Sports equipment at valuation	6 350	8 200

(a) Prepare a café account to show the profit or loss for the year ended 31 December 2018. **(5)**

(b) Prepare a subscriptions account to show the income for the year ended 31 December 2018. **(5)**

(c) Prepare an income and expenditure account for the year ended 31 December 2018. **(10)**

(d) Prepare a calculation of the accumulated fund at 1 January 2018. **(3)**

(e) Prepare a statement of financial position at 31 December 2018. **(9)**

(Total marks: 32)

Before you answer the question

There is a lot to do, so it is important to spend some time reading through the information given and thinking about how each item will be used. You may wish to pencil a note about details for the café account, the income and expenditure account, the final statement of financial position.

Don't forget to show workings for any more complex calculations.

Check your answer

4. (a)

Café account for the year ended 31 December 2018		
	$	$
Revenue		2 289 **(1)**
Less: cost of sales		
Opening inventory	890	
Purchases	1 392	**(1)**
	2 282	
Closing inventory	(970)	
		(1 312) **(1)**
		977
Less wages of café staff		(643) **(1)**
Profit for the year		334 **(1)**

(b)

Subscriptions account					
	$			$	
Income	8 880	**(1)**	Opening balance (received in advance)	280	**(1)**
Closing balance (received in advance) c/d	160		Receipts	8 420	**(1)**
			Closing balance (due) c/d	340	
	9 040			9 040	
Balance b/d	340	**(1)**	Balance b/d	160	**(1)**

(c)

Valeford Sports Club Income and expenditure account for the year ended 31 December 2018				
	$	$	$	
INCOME				
Subscriptions		8 880		**(1)**
Donations		800		**(1)**
Café profit		334		**(1)**
			10 014	
EXPENDITURE				
Rent of clubhouse and sports grounds ($2 200 **(1)** less $180 prepaid)		2 020		**(1)**
Wages of grounds staff ($2 835 **(1)** plus $120 due)		2 955		**(1)**
Loss on sports competitions				
Receipts	1 145			
Less competition prizes	(1 272)			
		127		**(1)**
Depreciation of sports equipment (W1)		1 650		
			(6 752)	
Surplus for year			3 262	**(1)**

W1 Depreciation of sports equipment: opening valuation $6 350 plus additions

$3 500 = $9 850 **(1)** less closing valuation $8 200 = $1 650   **(10)**

(d)

Accumulated fund at 1 January 2018		
	$	
Assets:		
Inventory	890	
Sports equipment	6 350	
Cash at bank	636	
	7 876	**(1)**
Less: liabilities		
Subscriptions received in advance	(280)	**(1)**
	7 596	**(1)**

(e)

Statement of financial position at 31 December 2018			
	$	$	
Non-current assets			
Sports equipment at valuation		8 200	**(1)**
Current assets			
Inventory	970		**(1)**
Other receivables: subscriptions due	340		**(1)**
rent prepaid	180		**(1)**
Cash at bank	1 448		**(1)**
		2 938	
Current liabilities			
Other payables: wages due	120		**(1)**
Subscriptions received in advance	160		**(1)**
		(280)	
		2 658	
		10 858	
Accumulated fund			
Balance 1 January		7 596	**(1)**
Add surplus for the year		3 262	**(1)**
		10 858	

 Common errors

Remember to:

- include the profit on the café in the income and expenditure account

- record the adjustments in the subscriptions account accurately

- combine the information about the sports competitions to provide a figure for the loss on this activity

- include and correctly calculate the depreciation charge in the income and expenditure account; provide workings for this figure

- provide a full title for the income and expenditure account and label the surplus for the year

- include the balance at bank when calculating the accumulated fund

- record the subscriptions due as a current asset and subscriptions received in advance as a current liability in the statement of financial position.

5. The following information about a company called G Limited is available for the year ended 31 December 2018.

	$
Carriage inwards	1 320
Direct wages	144 870
Electricity charges	4 480
Factory insurance	2 430
Factory machinery	
cost	85 000
provision for depreciation at 1 January 2018	39 000
Factory maintenance	2 980
Indirect wages and salaries	34 210
Inventories at 1 January 2018	
finished goods	17 590
raw materials	14 330
work in progress	3 800
Inventories at 31 December 2018	
finished goods	18 740
raw materials	13 260
work in progress	4 140
Office wages	22 980
Purchases of raw materials	102 770
Rent	25 200
Returns inwards	2 020
Returns outwards of raw materials	1 530
Revenue	428 370

Additional information:

- Direct wages were due but unpaid, $3,400 at 31 December 2018.
- Insurance was prepaid, $560, at 31 December 2018.
- Factory machinery should be depreciated by 20 per cent per annum using the reducing-balance method.
- Electricity charges and rent should be divided between the factory and offices in the ratio 3:1.

(a) Prepare a manufacturing account for the year ended 31 December 2018. **(17)**

(b) Prepare an income statement for the year ended 31 December 2018. **(10)**

(Total marks: 27)

Before you answer the question

Look carefully through the information, perhaps making a mental or written note about information for the manufacturing account and information for the income statement.

In the case of the manufacturing account you could also note which details will be recorded in the prime cost section and which items will be recorded in the factory overheads section.

Check your answer

5. (a)

G Limited Manufacturing account for the year ended 31 December 2018				
	$	$	$	
Opening inventory		14 330		(1)
Purchases	102 770			(1)
Less returns outwards	(1 530)			(1)
	101 240			
Carriage inwards	1 320			(1)
		102 560		
		116 890		
Less closing inventory		(13 260)		(1)
Cost of raw materials consumed			103 630	(1)
Direct wages ($144 870 + $3 400 due)			148 270	(1)
Prime cost			251 900	(1)
Factory overheads				
Electricity charges (¾ × $4 480)		3 360		(1)
Insurance ($2 430 – $560 prepaid)		1 870		(1)
Depreciation of machinery (W1)		9 200		(1)
Maintenance		2 980		(1)
Indirect wages and salaries		34 210		(1)
Rent (¾ × $25 200)		18 900		(1)
			70 520	
			322 420	
Adjustment for work in progress				
Opening inventory		3 800		(1)
Closing inventory		(4 140)		(1)
			(340)	
Cost of production			322 080	(1)

(b)

Income statement for the year ended 31 December 2018			
	$	$	
Revenue	428 370		
Less returns inwards	(2 020)		
		426 350	**(1)**
Opening inventory of finished goods	17 590		**(1)**
Cost of production	322 080		**(1)**
	339 670		
Less closing inventory of finished goods	(18 740)		**(1)**
Cost of sales of finished goods		(320 930)	**(1)**
Gross profit		105 420	**(1)**
Less expenses			
Electricity charges (¼ × $4 480)	1 120		**(1)**
Office wages	22 980		**(1)**
Rent (¼ × $25 200)	6 300		**(1)**
		(30 400)	
Profit for the year		75 020	**(1)**

⊗ Common errors

Remember to:

- include a full heading, labels for key items: cost of raw materials consumed, prime cost, etc.

- record factory overheads and non-factory expenses in the correct place

- divide expenses correctly between the factory overheads and the income statement

- record revenue in the income statement

- check which inventory values are recorded in the manufacturing account and which are recorded in the income statement

- retain factory overheads in the prime cost.

6. Waseem opened his retail business several years ago, but he has not kept a full set of accounting records. He purchases all goods for resale on credit, but sales are on both a credit and cash basis.

The following information is available about the business for the year ended 30 September 2018:

At 1 October 2017	$
Trade payables	17 800
Trade receivables	11 650
At 30 September 2018	
Trade payables	16 740
Trade receivables	13 130
Receipts	
Cash sales	77 400
Cheques received from trade receivables	129 520
Payments	
Cheques paid to trade payables	142 670

Waseem was able to claim cash discounts of $890 when settling the accounts of trade payables.

(a) Calculate the business's total sales for the year ended 30 September 2018. **(5)**

(b) Calculate the business's purchases for the year ended 30 September 2018. **(5)**

Waseem was unable to value his inventory on 30 September 2018. However, he is able to provide the following information.

Inventory at 1 October 2017	$13 820
Mark-up	$33\frac{1}{3}\%$

(c) Prepare the trading section of the income statement for the year ended 30 September 2018. Show clearly the value of the business's closing inventory. **(7)**

(Total marks: 17)

Before you answer the question

Incomplete records are a good test of your ability to select the right information at the right time. It is worthwhile checking all the details provided before you start the first task.

In tasks **(a)** and **(b)** it is possible to set out ledger accounts to find the credit sales and credit purchases, or to provide calculations instead. Choose whichever method you feel most comfortable with.

Check your answer

6. (a)

Dr				Total trade receivables			Cr
2017–18			$	**2017–18**		$	
Oct	1	Balance b/d	11 650 **(1)**	Oct–Sept	Bank	129 520	**(1)**
Oct–Sept		Credit sales	131 000 **(1)**	Sept 30	Balance c/d	13 130	
			142 650			142 650	
2018							
Oct	1	Balance b/d	13 130 **(1)**				

Alternative answer: use a calculation

	$	
Closing trade receivables	13 130	**(1)**
Less opening trade receivables	(11 650)	**(1)**
	1 480	
Add receipts from trade receivables	129 520	**(1)**
Credit sales	131 000	**(1)**

Total sales is credit sales $131 00 + cash sales $77 400 = $208 400 **(1)**

(b)

Dr				Total trade payables			Cr
2017–18			$	**2017–18**		$	
Oct–Sept		Bank	142 670 **(1)**	Oct 1	Balance b/d	17 800	**(1)**
		Discounts received	890 **(1)**	Oct–Sept 30	Purchases	142 500	**(1)**
Sept	30	Balance c/d	16 740				
			160 300			160 300	
				2018			
				Oct 1	Balance b/d	16 740	**(1)**

Alternative answer: using a calculation

	$	
Closing trade payables	16 740	**(1)**
Less opening trade payables	(17 800)	**(1)**
	(1 060)	
Add back amounts paid to trade payables	142 670	**(1)**
Add back discounts received	890	**(1)**
Credit purchases	142 500	**(1)**

(c)

Income statement (trading section) for year ended 30 September 2018			
	$	$	
Revenue from task (a)		208 400	**(1)**
Less cost of sales			
Opening inventory	23 430		**(1)**
Purchases from task (b)	142 500		**(1)**
	165 930		
Closing inventory	(9 630)		**(1)**
		(156 300)	**(1)**
Gross profit (25% see W1)		52 100	

W1 If the mark-up is 33⅓ percent (i.e. gross profit is 1 if cost of sales is 3 and revenue is 4); then gross margin is 25 per cent **(1)**; gross profit is 25% of revenue $208 400 = $52 100   **(1)**

 Common errors

Task **(a)**:

- forgetting to include cash sales in the final calculation

- making mistakes with the correct double entry, for example recording the opening balance as a credit entry in the ledger format; deducting the opening balance from the closing balance in the calculation method.

Task **(b)**:

- omitting the discounts received or recording this as a credit entry in the account rather than as a debit entry.

Task **(c)**:

- failing to convert the mark-up to gross margin and calculating gross profit as 20 per cent of revenue, rather than 25 per cent

- making an error in converting the mark-up to gross margin

- failing to label cost of sales and gross profit

- using abbreviations rather than a full heading.

Exam tip

1. Bring down the balance on the trade receivables and trade payables accounts – it is always good practice to do this on ledger accounts

2. Include appropriate narratives in the ledger accounts or in the calculations.

Multiple choice questions

1. A retailer's income statement includes the following details:

	$
Carriage outwards	3 000
Closing inventory	10 000
Goods taken for own use by the owner	1 000
Opening inventory	8 000
Purchases	60 000
Returns inwards	4 000
Revenue	95 000

   What was the business's cost of sales? (1)

   A $57 000   **B** $59 000   **C** $60 000   **D** $61 000

2. Which of the following should be included in other payables on a business's statement of financial position? (1)

   A accrued expenses and accrued income

   B accrued expenses and prepaid income

   C prepaid expenses and accrued income

   D prepaid expenses and prepaid income

3. A statement of financial position shows details of a business's current assets listed in order of liquidity.

   Which of the following is a correct sequence? (1)

   A inventory, trade receivables, other receivables, petty cash

   B other receivables, petty cash, inventory, trade receivables

   C petty cash, other receivables, trade receivables, inventory

   D trade receivables, inventory, petty cash, other receivables

4. Which of the following should be recorded on the debit side of a partner's current account? (1)

   A interest on capital

   B interest on a partner's loan

   C partnership salary

   D share of loss

5. Which of the following should be recorded in an appropriation account? (1)

	Interest on a partner's loan	Interest on capital	Partnership salary
A	✓	✓	
B		✓	✓
C	✓		✓
D		✓	

6. Cherry and Farad are in a partnership sharing profits and losses equally after charging interest on drawings. During a recent financial year the partnership made a profit of $12000. Interest on drawings was: Cherry $400; Farad, $600. What was Farad's net share of the profits? **(1)**

    A $5,400   **B** $5,900   **C** $6,600   **D** $7,100

7. Which of the following should not be shown in a statement of changes in equity? **(1)**

    A debenture interest

    B dividends paid

    C profit for the year

    D transfers to reserves

8. The directors of a company paid dividends on ordinary shares. In which of the company's financial statements should this be shown at the end of the financial year? **(1)**

	Income statement	Statement of changes in equity	Statement of financial position
A	No	No	Yes
B	No	Yes	No
C	Yes	No	No
D	Yes	Yes	Yes

9. Which statement best describes the paid-up share capital of a limited company? **(1)**

    A the amount that has been received from shareholders to date

    B the amount the directors have asked shareholders to pay

    C the number of shares the company has issued

    D the value of the issued share capital

10. A social club has recently purchased some new furniture. In which of the following financial statements will this appear? **(1)**

	Receipts and payments account	Income and expenditure account	Statement of financial position
A	✓	✓	✓
B	✓	✓	
C		✓	✓
D	✓		✓

11. A sports club received $9,200 in members' subscriptions in 2018. At 1 January 2018 subscriptions due but unpaid totalled $700 and at 31 December 2018 subscriptions received in advance totalled $900. What was the club's subscription income for 2018? **(1)**

    A $7,600   **B** $9,000   **C** $9,400   **D** $10800

12. Which of the following statements about a club's income and expenditure account is correct? **(1)**

   A   It includes capital expenditure.

   B   It includes loan repayments.

   C   It records amounts spent on repairs.

   D   It shows any improvement in cash funds.

13. A manufacturer provided the following information about production costs for a recent financial year.

	$ 000
Prime cost	510
Factory overheads	40
Decrease in value of inventories of work in progress during the year	10

What was the cost of production? **(1)**

   A $460 000   **B** $480 000   **C** $540 000   **D** $560 000

14. Which of the following is required when calculating prime cost? **(1)**

   A   carriage outwards   **C**   factory rent

   B   direct labour   **D**   indirect materials

15. A manufacturer provided the following information:

	$ 000
Opening inventory of finished goods	15
Closing inventory of finished goods	25
Goods taken for own use by owner	5
Cost of production	120

What is the manufacturer's cost of sales? **(1)**

   A $105 000   **B** $115 000   **C** $125 000   **D** $135 000

16. The following information is available about a business:

	$ 000
Capital, 1 January 2018	80
Capital, 31 December 2018	85
Drawings during year	16
Additional capital introduced in 2018	12

What was the business's profit or loss in 2018? **(1)**

   A   loss, $9,000

   B   loss, $1,000

   C   profit, $1,000

   D   profit, $9,000

17. A retailer does not keep full accounting records. The following information is available for December 2018:

	$
Trade payables, 1 December 2018	14 000
Trade payables, 31 December 2018	17 000
Payments to trade payables	20 000
Discounts received during	1 000

What was the business's credit purchases for December 2018? **(1)**

A $16 000   B $18 000   C $22 000   D $24 000

18. The trading section of a business's income statement records a cost of sales of $120 000.The business always obtained a gross margin of 33⅓ per cent. What was the business's revenue? **(1)**

A $150 000   B $160 000   C $180 000   D $200 000

(Total marks: 18)

Structured questions

1. Ajif is the owner of a business which provides office cleaning services for local businesses. On 31 March 2019 the following details were available for the year ended on that date.

(a) Describe the difference between the financial statements of a service business and a trading business referring to **i.** the income statement and **ii.** the statement of financial position. **(3)**

	$
Administration expenses	3 670
Cleaning equipment at valuation	2 980
Cleaning materials	1 830
Discounts allowed	210
Fees received from clients	67 920
Furniture and fittings	
cost	8 450
provision for depreciation at 1 April 2019	3 650
Insurance	1 050
Interest receivable	440
Irrecoverable debt written off	290
Motor vehicles	
cost	33 500
provision for depreciation at 1 April 2019	13 400
Profit on the disposal of some unwanted equipment	290
Staff wages	24 810

Additional information at 31 March 2019:

• There was an unpaid invoice for materials, $170.

• Cleaning equipment was revalued at $2,550.

• Insurance includes cover of $480 for the four months ending 30 June 2019.

• Interest receivable of $40 is accrued.

- A provision for doubtful debts of $310 is to be created.

- Depreciation should be provided on other non-current assets as follows:

  - furniture and fittings at 15 per cent per annum using the reducing-balance method

  - motor vehicles at 20 per cent per annum using the straight-line method.

(b) Prepare the income statement for the year ended 31 March 2019. **(14)**

(Total marks: 17)

2. The following balances remained in the books of Hillside Wholesalers at 28 February 2019 after completion of the income statement for the year ended on that date:

	$ 000
Accrued interest receivable	2
Accrued salaries	11
Bank loan (repayable 2021)	22
Capital	673
Cash at bank	43
Delivery vehicles	
cost	88
provision for depreciation	35
Drawings	29
Furniture and equipment	
cost	29
provision for depreciation	9
Inventory	53
Loss for the year	17
Petty cash in hand	1
Premises	
cost	485
provision for depreciation	31
Prepaid insurance	3
Prepaid rent receivable	4
Provision for doubtful debts	5
Trade payables	62
Trade receivables	102

Prepare the statement of financial position at 28 February 2019. **(13)**

3. Amy and Winston are considering forming a partnership. They have agreed that Amy will be responsible for the day-to-day management of the business. They realize that they would have more capital available as a result of forming a partnership. Fixed capitals are planned to be: Amy $80 000; Winston $70 000.

(a) State two advantages which could arise from forming a partnership, other than having more capital available. **(2)**

Amy and Winston have decided to prepare a formal partnership agreement which will provide for 12 per cent per annum interest on capitals, a partnership salary for Amy of $9,000, and equal shares of remaining profits and losses.

(b) Explain why Amy and Winston are wise to prepare a formal partnership agreement. **(2)**

(c) Explain why the partnership agreement should include a salary for Amy. **(2)**

The partners had considered including interest on drawings in the partnership agreement.

(d) State one possible benefit of including interest on drawings in a partnership agreement. **(1)**

The partnership made a profit of $24 000 in its first year.

(e) Prepare a detailed calculation of Amy's share of the profit for the first year. **(4)**

During the year Winston withdrew $15 200 for private use.

(f) Prepare Winston's current account for the first year in the business. Balance the account at the year end. **(4)**

(g) Interpret the closing balance of Winston's current account. **(1)**

(Total marks: 16)

4. Paloma and Salman are in partnership sharing profits and losses equally. Their partnership agreement includes the following terms.

- Salman is entitled to receive interest on his loan at 5 per cent per annum.

- Interest on total drawings should be charged at 10 per cent.

- Each partner should receive interest on fixed capitals at 8 per cent per annum.

- Paloma should receive an annual salary of $15 000.

The following information has been extracted from the partnership's books of account for the year ended 30 September 2018:

	$
Administration expenses	3 640
Capital accounts	
Paloma	90 000
Salman	70 000
Carriage outwards	1 430
Drawings	
Paloma	23 200
Salman	17 800
Furniture and equipment	
at cost	50 000
provision for depreciation, 1 October 2017	18 000
Insurance	3 410
Inventory, 1 October 2017	14 440
Loan from Salman	18 000
Purchases	83 450
Returns inwards	830
Revenue	139 910
Wages	29 620

Additional information:

- Inventory at 30 September 2018 was valued at $11 250.

- Insurance, costing $290, was prepaid at 30 September 2018.

- Wages due but unpaid totalled $430 at 30 September 2018.

- Depreciation should be provided on furniture and equipment at the rate of 20 per cent per annum using the reducing-balance method.

   (a) Prepare an income statement for the year ended 30 September 2018. **(15)**

   (b) Prepare an appropriation account for the year ended 30 September 2018. **(9)**

   (Total marks: 24)

5. P Limited has an issued share capital of 900 000 shares of $1 each, 120 000 6 per cent redeemable preference shares of $1 each. All shares are fully paid. The company also issued 6 per cent debentures (2026) issued some years ago and raised $250 000.

   (a) Describe two ways in which ordinary shares differ from debentures. **(4)**

   (b) Explain why it is important to know whether preference shares are redeemable or non-redeemable when preparing a company's financial statements. **(2)**

The following information is available for the year ended 30 September 2018:

	$
Administrative expenses	53 700
Cost of sales	299 400
Debenture interest	15 000
Distribution expenses	49 600
General reserve at 1 October 2017	85 000
Retained earnings at 1 October 2017	97 700
Revenue	537 200

Additional information:

- Directors' remuneration of $4,500 is accrued at 30 September 2018.

- Directors' remuneration is charged to administrative expenses.

- Distribution expenses of $1,800 were prepaid at 30 September 2018.

- The directors paid the preference share dividend during the year and a dividend of $0.10 per share on the ordinary shares.

- The directors agreed to transfer $42 000 to the general reserve at 30 September 2018.

(c) Prepare the income statement for the year ended 30 September 2018. **(11)**

(d) Prepare the statement of changes in equity at 30 September 2018. **(6)**

(Total marks: 23)

6. The following balances remained in the books of C Limited at 31 December 2018 after the preparation of the company's income statement for the year ended on that date:

	$ 000
7% debentures (2028)	150
Cash at bank	23
Dividends paid	75
General reserve	110
Inventory	34
Issued share capital: 750 000 ordinary shares of $1 each	750
Non-current assets	
cost	1 225
provision for depreciation	137
Other payables	9
Other receivables	6
Profit for the year	146
Retained earnings	56
Trade payables	27
Trade receivables	22

The directors have agreed to transfer 60 000 to the general reserve.

(a) Define the term 'equity'. **(2)**

(b) Describe the main difference between called-up share capital and paid-up share capital. **(2)**

(c) Prepare the statement of changes in equity at 31 December 2018. **(6)**

(d) Prepare the statement of financial position at 31 December 2018. **(11)**

(Total marks: 21)

7. (a) Describe the purpose of a receipts and payments account. **(2)**

The Friendship Social Club's main source of income is members' subscriptions.

The club's treasurer has provided the following information:

- The annual member's subscription is $40.

- At 31 December 2017, six members had not paid their subscriptions for 2017, but four members had paid their subscription for 2018 in advance.

- During 2018, 150 subscriptions were received, including the subscriptions outstanding from 2017.

- At 31 December 2018, seven members had not paid their subscriptions for 2018, but three members had paid their subscription for 2018.

(b) Prepare a subscriptions account to show the club's income for 2018. **(6)**

(c) Define the term 'accumulated fund'. **(2)**

(Total marks: 10)

8. The treasurer of the Outreach Tennis Club is about to prepare an income and expenditure account for the year ended 31 December 2018.

Assets and liabilities at 1 January 2018 included the following:

	$
Club premises and grounds at net book value	85 000
Tennis equipment at valuation	11 900
Inventory of refreshments	830
Subscriptions due	1 840
Subscriptions received in advance	360

Receipts and payments account for the year ended 31 December 2018				
Receipts	$	Payments	$
Opening balance b/d	510	Suppliers of refreshments	3 160
Members' subscriptions	11 420	Competition prizes	1 100
Gifts from members	880	General expenses	6 420
Proceeds from the sale of tennis equipment	1 860	Wages of groundsmen	7 790
Refreshment sales	4 230	Electricity charges	1 230
Ticket sales for competitions	1 470	Closing balance c/d	670
	20 370		20 370
Balance b/d	670		

The following information was available at 31 December 2018:

- $380 was owed to suppliers of refreshments.

- Inventory of unsold refreshments was valued at $620.

- The tennis equipment sold during the year was valued at $2,400.

- Some prizes valued at $140 were being retained for competitions to be held in 2019.

- General expenses due but unpaid were $220.

- Subscriptions due but unpaid were $1,520.

- Subscriptions received in advance were $480.

- Premises are to be depreciated by $400.

- Tennis equipment was valued at $8,240.

(a) Prepare an account to show the profit or loss on refreshments for the year ended 31 December 2018. **(5)**

(b) Prepare an income and expenditure account for the year ended 31 December 2018. **(13)**

The treasurer will inform members that it will be necessary to buy new tennis equipment for $6,000 early in 2019.

(c) Suggest four ways the club could raise the funds necessary to purchase the new sports equipment. **(4)**

(Total marks: 22)

9. Ephraim is a manufacturer of children's toys.

(a) Describe the purpose of a manufacturing account. **(2)**

(b) Define 'prime cost'. **(1)**

Ephraim has provided the following details for the financial year ended 31 December 2018:

	$
Administrative expenses	11 420
Advertising	1 320
Depreciation of factory machinery	18 900
Discounts received	390
Factory indirect materials	420
Factory manager's salary	21 430
Factory insurance	3 960
Finance costs	860
Purchases of finished goods	5 410
Purchases of raw materials	86 300
Returns outwards	3 720
Revenue	302 730
Selling expenses	4 480
Wages of production staff	56 370

	Raw materials	Work in progress	Finished goods
	$	$	$
1 January 2018	28 500	7 320	17 450
31 December 2018	32 400	6 190	15 240

Additional information:

- Factory insurance $440 was prepaid at 31 December 2018.

- Administration expenses $190 were accrued at 31 December 2018.

(c) Prepare the manufacturing account for the year ended 31 December 2018. **(14)**

(d) Prepare the income statement for the year ended 31 December 2018. **(13)**

(Total marks: 30)

10. Haroon has provided the following details for his manufacturing business for the year ended 30 September 2018:

	$
Prime cost	349 200
Factory overheads	111 650
Work in progress	
1 October 2017	14 270
30 September 2018	17 530

(a) Calculate the business's cost of production for the year ended 30 September 2018. **(2)**

(b) State the meaning of the term 'work in progress'. **(2)**

The following additional information has also been provided for the year ended 30 September 2018:

	$
Administrative expenses	9 930
Depreciation of office non-current assets	6 450
Distribution expenses	11 940
Goods taken for own use by owner	4 520
Provision for doubtful debts at 1 October 2017	780
Returns inwards	3 170
Revenue	592 600

Distribution expenses $280 were prepaid at 30 September 2018. It has been decided to decrease the provision for doubtful debts by $180 at 31 December 2018.

The value of other inventories was as follows:

	1 October 2017	30 September 2018
	$	$
Finished goods	9 400	12 800
Raw materials	11 100	9 200

(c) Prepare the income statement for the year ended
30 September 2018. **(12)**

(d) Prepare an extract from the statement of financial position at
30 September 2018 to show inventories. **(4)**

(Total marks: 20)

11. Anais opened her wholesale business on the 1 October 2017 with a capital
contribution of $45 000. She has not kept full accounting records.

(a) Describe two possible problems for a business which does
not have full accounting records. **(4)**

Anais has been able to provide the following information about her
business's assets and liabilities at 30 September 2018:

	$
Bank overdraft	3 270
Bank loan (repayable 2020)	14 200
Cash in hand	460
Furniture and equipment	8 880
Inventory	22 410
Motor vehicles	28 500
Rent of premises paid in advance	330
Trade payables	11 960
Trade receivables	8 420
Wages due but unpaid	720

During the year ended 30 September 2018 Anais made an additional
capital contribution of $6,000, but she withdrew $18 500 for private use,
and also took goods for her own use, to the value of $1,700.

(b) Prepare a statement of affairs at 30 September 2018 and identify
the business's capital at that date. **(11)**

(c) Calculate the business's profit or loss for the year ended
30 September 2018. **(6)**

(d) State two items of additional information required if Anais
wished to know her business's total sales for the year ended
30 September 2018. **(2)**

(Total marks: 23)

12. Iqbal is a retailer who purchases goods for resale on credit, but sells goods
on a strictly cash basis. He has not maintained full accounting records.

The following details are available about the year ended 30 June 2018:

	$
Trade payables, 1 July 2017	14 950
Trade payables, 30 June 2018	16 120
Payments to trade payables	151 370
Discounts received	2 440

(a) Calculate Iqbal's credit purchases for the year ended 30 June 2016. **(5)**

Additional information:

	at 1 July 2017	at 30 June 2018
	$	$
Cash in hand	260	370
Equipment net book value	14 100	?
Inventory	8 560	16 310

Details taken from bank statements for the year ended 30 June 2018:

	$
Receipts	
Cash takings banked	138 300
Proceeds from sale of unwanted equipment	1 420
Payments	
General expenses	2 450
Rent	8 200

Iqbal has totalled till rolls which show cash sales totalled $195 400 during the year ended 30 June 2018. Cash was used to pay wages of $28 450. Any missing cash was taken for his own private use.

(b) Prepare a cash account for the year ended 30 June 2018 and identify the amount of Iqbal's drawings. **(12)**

Additional information:

- The equipment disposed of during the year ending 30 June 2018 had a net book value of $1,300.

- Equipment should be depreciated by $1,500.

- Wages of $580 were due but unpaid at 30 June 2018.

- Rent includes a payment of $1,500 for the quarter ended 31 July 2018.

(c) Prepare an income and expenditure account for the year ended 30 June 2018. **(12)**

(Total marks: 29)

Unit 6:
Analysis and interpretation

Unit outline

Owners and managers of businesses will pay considerable attention to how well their businesses are performing so that they can take steps to overcome any weaknesses and put in place plans to build on financial strengths. Often they compare the performance of their own business with the results for previous years and, where available, the results for other similar businesses.

This unit introduces the techniques used to analyse and evaluate performance.

Either tick these boxes to build a record of your revision, or use them to identify your strengths and weaknesses.

Your revision checklist

Specification	Theme	🙂	😐	🙁
6.1 Calculating ratios	6.1.1 The importance of ratios and profitability ratios			
	6.1.2 Liquidity ratios			
6.2 Interpretation of accounting ratios	6.2.1 Comparing results for different years			
	6.2.2 Users of accounting information; limitations of inter-firm comparisons and financial statements			

You will need to know how to:

- calculate and explain gross margin, profit margin and return on capital employed
- use and discuss current ratio and liquid (acid test) ratio
- calculate and explain rate of inventory turnover (times), trade receivables turnover (days) and trade payables turnover (days).

6.1.1 Importance of ratios and profitability ratios

Importance of ratios

Ratios are a means of analysing and comparing the performance of a business. They:

- are used to compare the results of a business overs several years
- are used to compare the results of similar businesses
- enable significant factors of performance to be highlighted.

Profitability ratios

Ratio	Formula	Explanation
Gross margin	Gross profit × 100	• Measures how much gross profit is made is made per $100 of sales
Profit margin	Revenue	• Measures how much profit for the year is made per $100 of sales
Return on **capital employed**	Profit for the year × 100	• Measures how much profit for the year is made per $100 of capital employed

These ratios are all expressed as percentages.

✏️ **Apply**

1. A business has revenue of $800 000, cost of sales of $600 000 and total expenses of $120 000. Calculate:

   (a) gross margin

   (b) profit margin.

2. A business made a profit for the year ending 31 December 2018 of $96 000. On that date the business had capital of $460 000 and non-current liabilities of $50 000. Calculate the return on capital employed.

⏪ **Recap**

1. Ratios are an important means of assessing how well businesses are performing.

2. There are three ratios used to measure the profitability of a business.

3. Each of the ratios is expressed as a percentage.

4. The ratios become useful for a business when comparisons are made over several years or when comparisons are made with similar businesses.

⏱️ **Review**

There is more about profitability ratios in section 6.1 of *Essential Accounting for Cambridge IGCSE® & O Level (third edition)*, pages 294–6.

6.1.2 Liquidity ratios

Ratio	Formula	Explanation
Current ratio (sometimes referred to as the working capital ratio)	Current assets: current liabilities	• Measures whether there are sufficient liquid funds to meet all the business's obligations as they fall due in the medium term. • Obligations include all the causes of cash outflows: paying suppliers, paying expenses, providing for drawings, etc. • The ratio is expressed in the form ×:1, e.g. 1.5:1 (where there is 1.5 times as many current assets as current liabilities).
Liquid (acid test) ratio	Current assets less inventory: current liabilities	• Measures whether there are sufficient liquid funds to meet all the business's obligations as they fall due in the short term. • The omission of inventory means that only current assets which can be turned into cash in the near future are considered. • Current assets without inventory is sometimes referred to as liquid assets. • The ratio is also expressed in the form ×:1.
Rate of inventory turnover	$\dfrac{\text{Cost of sales}}{\text{Average inventory}}$	• Measures how quickly a business is selling its inventory. • The ratio is expressed as so many times, e.g. eight times (means the average inventory is sold eight times in a year).
Trade receivables turnover	$\dfrac{\text{Trade receivables} \times 365}{\text{Credit sales}}$	• Measures how quickly credit customers are settling their accounts. • The ratio is expressed as so many day, e.g. 31 days (means credit customers are settling their accounts on average 31 days after the credit sale taking place). • It is usual to round up the ratio (e.g. 31.3 days would be recorded as 32 days).
Trade payables turnover	$\dfrac{\text{Trade payables} \times 365}{\text{Credit purchases}}$	• Measures how quickly credit suppliers are paid. • The ratio is expressed in days, e.g. 33 days. • It is usual to round the ratio up to the nearest whole number.

✎ Apply

3. On 31 December 2018 a business has current assets of $84 000; this includes inventory valued at $49 000. The business has current liabilities of $23 000. Calculate:

   (a) current ratio (to 2 decimal places)

   (b) liquid (acid test) ratio (to 2 decimal places).

4. A business's income statement includes the following details: revenue $920 000, gross profit $460 000, opening inventory $21 000, closing inventory $25 000. Calculate the rate of inventory turnover.

5. A business's financial statements include the following details: revenue $836 000, purchases $456 000, trade receivables $41 400, trade payables $37 900. Cash sales account for 40 per cent of all sales; all purchases are on credit. Calculate:

   (a) trade receivables turnover

   (b) trade payables turnover.

◀◀ Recap

1. There are five ratios used to measure a business's liquidity.

2. The current ratio and liquid (acid test) ratios measure how well a business can turn assets into cash in order to meet its day-to-day obligations.

3. The rate of inventory turnover measures how quickly a business's average inventory is sold and replaced.

4. The trade receivables turnover and trade payables turnover measure in days how quickly the accounts of credit customers and credit payables are settled.

⏱ Review

There is more about liquidity ratios in section 6.1 of *Essential Accounting for Cambridge IGCSE® & O Level (third edition)*, pages 294–6.

You will need to know how to:

- prepare and comment on simple statements showing comparison of results for different years
- make recommendations and suggestions for improving profitability and working capital
- explain the difference between gross margin and profit margin as an indicator of a business's efficiency
- explain the relationship of gross profit and profit for the year to the valuation of inventory, rate of inventory turnover, revenue, expenses and equity
- explain the problems of inter-firm comparisons and apply accounting ratios to them
- describe interested parties
- explain the limitations of accounting statements.

6.2.1 Comparing results for different years

Investigating profitability ratios

Ratio	Possible problems	How ratios might be improved	Examples of possible drawbacks
Gross margin	Lower selling prices to make the business more competitive	Increasing selling price	Could make the business uncompetitive
	Increases in the cost of goods being sold which have not been passed on to customers	Finding cheaper suppliers	Could result in a lower quality of product which could deter customers
Profit margin	Reduced gross margin arising from problems listed above	Increasing gross margin (see above)	See above
	Increase in expenses and/or new expenses incurred	Reducing expenditure on running costs	Could affect the efficiency at which the business operates if reductions are too drastic
	Loss of sources of income	Finding other sources of income	May not be possible, or may distract owner(s) from the business's main purpose
Return on capital employed	Profits have decreased	Improving profits (see above)	See above
	Capital employed has increased; new resources have not produced sufficient additional profit	Reducing the value of the capital employed	May affect the business's normal operations if reduction in resources is too drastic

Investigating liquidity ratios which are weaker than they should be

Gross profit = sales revenue − cost of sales. Therefore, the gross margin percentage can only be affected by changes to cost of sales or sales revenue.

Profit = gross profit + income − expenses. Therefore, the profit margin can only be affected by changes to gross profit, income and expenses.

The valuation of inventory will have an effect on the cost of sales. Therefore, changes in the valuation of inventory will have an impact on gross margin.

A change in revenue will have an impact on gross profit assuming that cost of sales does not change to the same degree. This will have an impact on gross margin.

Where liquidity ratios are stronger than they need to be

It is possible for some liquidity ratios to be stronger compared to what is regarded as normal for the type of business under review.

Ratio	Possible problems	How ratios might be improved	Examples of possible drawbacks
Current ratio	Finding it more difficult to make payments on time Loss of cash discounts Credit suppliers refuse further credit Unable to take advantage of favourable opportunities	• Introduce additional capital • Take out a long-term loan • Reduce drawing • Sell off surplus non-current assets • Increase profits	• Loan interest will reduce profits • Loan will require repayment affecting liquidity at a future date • Owner may not be able to provide additional capital • Owner may not be able to afford to reduce drawings
Liquid (acid test) ratio	See above	• Reduce levels of inventory • Buy cheaper goods	• May not be able to provide the range of goods expected by customers • Risk of running out of some items if demand changes unexpectedly • Possible reduction in quality may result in loss of customers
Rate of inventory turnover	Falling profits as inventory is sold less quickly Increase in storage costs as quantity of unsold goods increases	• Reduce levels of inventory • Increase spending on advertising • Reduce selling prices	• May not be able to provide the range of goods expected by customers • Risk of running out of some items if demand changes unexpectedly • Increase in expenses reducing profits • May not increase demand sufficiently so profits fall
Trade payables turnover	Loss of cash discounts when payments delayed Interest charged by suppliers on overdue accounts Loss of credit terms Suppliers refuse to accept further orders	• Increase cash available by reducing time given for credit customers to pay • Increase cash available by reducing spending on running costs • Delay spending on improvements to non-current assets • Increase bank overdraft	• Any cash discounts given to credit customers will reduce profits • Reducing spending on running costs or non-current assets could make business more inefficient • Interest charges on bank overdraft will reduce profits
Trade receivables turnover	Credit customers delay settlement of their accounts Delays in receiving cash from credit customers leads to difficulties in meeting other commitments	• Offer cash discounts to prompt earlier settlement of accounts • Charge interest on overdue accounts • Improve credit control systems • Refuse new orders from credit customers whose accounts are overdue	• Cash discounts will reduce profits • Tightening of credit control and refusal to take more orders may lead to a loss of sales if credit customers decide to buy from competitors

Current ratio is too high: indicates that the business has too many resources tied up as current assets
• Levels of inventory could be unnecessarily high.
• This could lead to high storage costs.
• There is the possibility of more wastage as items become out of date.
Liquid (acid test) ratio is too high: indicates that the business has too many liquid assets
• Payments to credit suppliers could be delayed, resulting in the loss of cash discounts and possibly damaging relationships.
• The business could have unnecessarily high levels of cash resources which could have been used to improve the business.
Trade payables turnover is too low: indicates that credit suppliers are being paid sooner than required
• There could be less cash available to make other payments.
Trade receivables turnover is too high: indicates that credit customers are being required to pay more quickly than normal.
• The business could lose credit sales if credit customers decide to seek better credit terms elsewhere.
• Too many cash discounts could have been allowed, reducing profits and cash inflows.

 Recap

1. Weak profitability and liquidity ratios can be remedied, but sometimes the actions taken can have adverse effects.

2. Where a business has a lower current ratio and liquid (acid test) ratio than expected it could lead to difficulties in making payments when due.

3. The current ratio and liquid (acid test) ratio can be too high, which indicates that the business has too high levels of current assets and is wasting resources.

4. If credit suppliers are paid sooner than necessary this could lead to a lack of liquid funds to make other payments.

5. If trade receivables are required to be paid sooner than normal, they could take their custom elsewhere.

Apply

1. The owner of a business wishes to improve the gross margin. Identify two actions the owner could take.

2. The owner of a business intends to improve the business revenue by paying for an advertising campaign. Do you advise the owner to go ahead with this proposal? Justify your advice.

3. State **two** ways in which the owner of a business could improve the business's current ratio.

4. State one problem which could arise if a business's liquid (acid test) ratio is:

    (a) too low

    (b) too high.

5. Explain **one** way in which a business could improve its rate of inventory turnover.

6. Describe **two** possible consequences of allowing the trade receivables turnover to increase.

Review

There is more information about interpreting accounting statements in sections 6.2–6.5 of *Essential Accounting for Cambridge IGCSE® & O Level (third edition)*, pages 301–7.

6.2.2 Users of accounting information; limitations of inter-firm comparisons and financial statements

Users of accounting information

The main function of accounting statements is to provide useful information for those who are affected by a business's performance. These groups are referred to as 'interested parties' or 'stakeholders'.

Interested party	Examples of concerns
Internal users: those who are operating within the business	
Owners	• Profit made by the business • Liquidity of the business • Level of drawings which can be sustained • Whether to invest more in the business
Manager(s)	• Profitability and liquidity of the business • Effect of current performance on future planning and decisions
External users: those who are operating from outside the business	
Trade payables	• Ability of the business to pay on time, i.e. the business's liquidity position • Likelihood of continued trading and repeat orders
Banks and other lenders	• Ability of the business to make regular interest payments and loan repayments, i.e. the business's liquidity position • Ability of a business to offer security for any loan when a loan application is made
Investors	• What are the risks involved in investing in a business based on the business's profitability, liquidity, opportunities for continued growth, etc.? • Will there be a regular return on investment which requires an assessment of profitability and liquidity?
Club members	• Is the club financially viable so that it will continue in existence? • Is it likely that the club's facilities will be maintained or improved?
Government	• Is the business making a contribution to the economy: offering employment, making profits and so making tax payments?
Tax authorities	• Is the business making accurate tax assessments? • Is the business in a position to pay taxes when due?

Internal users (owners and managers) will have full access to the financial records of the business.

Some external users (such as credit suppliers, potential investors) may not always have access to the financial statements of a sole trader or partnership.

There are other potential interested parties to consider: employees, competitors, the general public, customers, etc.

Limitations of inter-firm comparisons and accounting statements

As well comparing the results of a business over several years, it can be useful to compare the results of a business with those of a similar business. It is important that comparisons are only made with a business which is in the same industry. However, this process may not be straightforward, for the reasons explored in the table below.

Limitation	Example
The financial statements of a similar business could be based on quite **different accounting policies**	<ul><li>Different depreciation may be used</li><li>There may be different depreciation rates</li><li>Different methods may be used to value inventory</li><li>Different pricing policies may be used</li><li>Different means may be used to measure performance, such as using a different formula for calculating return on capital employed</li></ul>
The similar business may have a **different year end**	<ul><li>Levels of inventory will vary depending on the time of the year</li></ul>
Similar businesses could be **financed or resourced quite differently**	<ul><li>One business may be financed by capital and long-term loans; but another business could rely on capital only</li><li>One business may rent premises, affecting profit levels; another business may own premises, affecting levels of capital invested</li><li>One business could hire motor vehicles and equipment, affecting the income statement; another business could own its own motor vehicles and equipment, affecting levels of capital invested</li></ul>
Inflation is ignored in preparing financial statements	<ul><li>One business could have been established many years ago when price levels were much lower; another business could have been established recently when prices were higher due to inflation</li></ul>
Non-monetary items are not recorded in financial statements	<ul><li>One business may have a highly motivated workforce and highly effective management; another business could be subject to labour disputes and inefficient management processes</li></ul>
Lack of information in financial statements	<ul><li>It will not be clear whether inventory levels shown on a statement of financial position are typical</li><li>It will not be clear which depreciation methods and rates have been used</li><li>It may not be known if one of the businesses in the comparison has been affected by a serious event causing temporary closure, such as a fire</li><li>It may not be known that a business's profit has been unusually large because of a one-off project which proved to be very successful</li></ul>

Recap

1. There are many interested parties who will wish to assess a business's performance.

2. Interested parties are usually divided into two groups: internal users and external users.

3. When assessing a business's performance it is important to remember that accounting statements have limitations – most notably they only record financial information.

4. Non-financial details could be of considerable importance in making a valid assessment of a business's performance.

5. Inter-firm comparisons can be very helpful in assessing how well a business is doing, but there could be reasons why comparisons with a similar business may not be altogether valid.

 Apply

7. Identify **three** external interested parties who would wish to review the performance of a business.

8. The member of a club has been told that the membership subscription will be increased by 25 per cent in the next financial year. Identify **three** factors about the club which would mean the member will be content to pay the increased membership subscription.

9. Identify **four** factors you would wish to check before you could be sure that an inter-firm comparison of performance is valid.

Review

There is more about interested parties and difficulties making inter-firm comparisons in section 6.5 of *Essential Accounting for Cambridge IGCSE® & O Level (third edition)*, on page 307.

Exam-style questions

1. Anna, a retailer, uses ratio analysis. She has provided the following information about her business:

Summarized income statement for the year ended 31 December 2018		
	$	$
Revenue		630 000
Opening inventory	17 500	
Purchases	407 000	
	424 500	
Closing inventory	(24 500)	
Cost of sales		420 000
Gross profit		210 000
Expenses		(126 500)
Profit for the year		83 500

Statement of financial position at 31 December 2018		
Assets	$	$
Non-current assets at net book value		560 000
Current assets		
Inventory	24 500	
Trade receivables	25 800	
Cash at bank	12 200	
		62 500
Total assets		662 500
Capital		
Opening balance	447 700	
Profit for the year	83 500	
	531 200	
Less drawings	(28 600)	
		502 600
Non-current liabilities		
Bank loan		75 000
Current liabilities		
Trade payables		24 900
Total capital and liabilities		662 500

Additional information:

- Credit sales accounted for 50 per cent of all sales.

- Credit purchases accounted for 80 per cent of all purchases.

(a) Give two reasons why using ratio analysis is beneficial to Anna's company. **(2)**

(b) Calculate the following ratios: **(14)**

  i. gross margin

  ii. profit margin

  iii. return on capital employed

  iv. current ratio

  v. liquid (acid test) ratio

  vi. rate of inventory turnover

  vii. trade receivables turnover

  viii. trade payables turnover. **(Total marks: 16)**

Before you answer the question

Remember it is recommended that you provide more information than just the answer when calculating ratios. Include, for example, details of the formula and the information selected from the financial statements.

Exam tip

As always, when you have checked your answer, spend a little time making corrections and making notes about what you should have done. This will ensure you get the most out of your work on this question.

Check your answer

1. **(a)** Ratio analysis will help Anna assess the performance **(1)** of her business, it will highlight possible strengths and weaknesses **(1)** in profitability and liquidity.

(b)

i.	Gross margin	Gross profit × 100 / Revenue	**(1)**	$210 000 x 100 = 33.33% / $630 000	**(1)**
ii.	Profit margin	Profit for the year × 100 / Revenue	**(1)**	$83 500 x 100 = 13.25% / $630 000	**(1)**
iii.	*Return on capital employed**	Profit for the year × 100 / Capital employed	**(1)**	$83 500 x 100 = 16.61% / $502 600	**(1)**
iv.	Current ratio	CA:CL	**(1)**	$62 500:$24 900 = 2.51:1	**(1)**
v.	Liquid (acid test) ratio	Current assets less inventory: CL	**(1)**	$38 000:$24 900 = 1.53:1	**(1)**
vi.	Rate of inventory turnover	Cost of sales / Average inventory	**(1)**	$420 000 = 20 times / $21 000	**(1)**
vii.	Trade receivable days	Trade receivables × 365 / Credit sales	**(1)**	$25 8000 x 365 = 30 days / $315 000	**(1)**
viii.	Trade payable days	Trade payables × 365 / Credit purchases	**(1)**	$24 900 x 365 = 28 days / $325 600	**(1)**

*Capital employed could be based on the opening capital + non-current liabilities.

Common errors

Remember to:

- give details of the formula used

- use the correct formula

- show details of the information extracted from the financial statements

- extract the correct details from the financial statements

- label each answer in the correct format, i.e. %, x:y: time, days

- work to 2 decimal places for some of the ratios shown (the question may ask for a different number of decimal places)

- round up the days for trade receivables turnover and trade payables turnover.

2. Samir owns Horizon Retail Stores. He has been comparing his business's performance comparing the results for 2018 with those for 2017. He has provided the following information:

	2017	2018
Gross margin	45%	40%
Profit margin	11%	13%
Return on capital employed	14%	11%
Current ratio	1.8:1	2.1:1
Trade payables turnover	33 days	29 days

Additional information:

The usual current ratio for this type of business is 2.0:1.

(a) State **two** reasons why the gross margin may have decreased from 2017 to 2018. **(2)**

(b) Explain **two** reasons why the profit margin may have increased from 2017 to 2018. **(4)**

(c) Explain **one** reason why the return on capital employed has decreased from 2017 to 2018. **(1)**

Samir is pleased with the change in the current ratio comparing 2018 with 2017.

(d) Advise Samir whether he should be pleased with the change in the current ratio. Justify your answer. **(5)**

Samir notes that the trade payables turnover ratio has decreased from 2017 to 2018.

(e) i. State **one** benefit of the decrease in this ratio. **(1)**

ii. State **one** drawback on the decrease in this ratio. **(1)**

(Total marks: 14)

Before you answer the question

Check the information provided carefully.

Look at the change in each ratio and decide whether the change represents an improvement or a decline in the business's performance.

Make sure you are comparing 2018 with 2017 (rather than 2017 with 2018).

Check your answer

2. **(a)** Selling prices were lower **(1)**; the cost of purchases increased **(1)**.

(b) Profit margin may have increased because the business was run more efficiently **(1)** expenses were reduced (for example there was a reduction in part-time hours for shop assistants/similar example **(1)**. Incidental income could have increased **(1)**, for example Samir could have rented out some unused space at the business premises/similar example **(1)**.

(c) Return on capital employed may have decreased because there was an increase in the value of capital + non-current liabilities **(1)**. Perhaps the owner has invested more capital/the business has taken out a long-term loan **(1)**.

(d) Advice: (either agree or disagree). **(1)**

The ratio is better because the current ratio is higher than last year **(1)** and this will mean that Samir can pay amounts due more easily **(1)**.

However, the ratio is now higher than the average for this type of business **(1)** and this means that he has some funds which are unnecessarily tied up as current assets, so wasting resources **(1)**.

(e) i. Benefit: Samir may receive more cash discounts or discounts received. **(1)**

ii. Drawback: less cash will be available for other payments. **(1)**

Multiple choice questions

1. At the end of its financial year a business had non-current assets of $60 000, working capital of $10 000, non-current liabilities of $20 000 and it had made a profit for the year of $20 000. What was the business's return on capital employed (to 2 decimal places)? **(1)**

A 25.00%   C 40.00%

B 28.57%   D 66.67%

2. A sole trader has provided the following details:

	$
Opening inventory	24 000
Purchases	100 000
Revenue	152 000
Closing inventory	16 000

What is the business's rate of inventory turnover? **(1)**

A 2.7 times   C 5.4 times

B 3.8 times   D 7.6 times

3. A business's financial statements included the following details: bank overdraft $2,000, inventory $9,000, trade payables $5,000, trade receivables $8,000. What was the business's liquid (acid test) ratio? **(1)**

A 5.8:1   C 2.0:1

B 2.4:1   D 1.1:1

4. The owner of a business wishes to improve the trade receivable turnover. What action should the owner take? **(1)**

A decrease selling prices   C offer credit customers a cash discount

B increase selling prices   D sell more goods on credit

Common errors

- Where the question asks you to 'state', there is no need to answer in too much detail – a concise phrase or sentence is all that is required.

- Where the task is to 'explain', provide a clear answer with some development to demonstrate full understanding.

- In **(b)**, note that improved gross margin was not the reason for higher profits – the gross margin actually declined.

- In **(e)**, remember to cover reasons for agreeing and reasons for disagreeing.

- In **(e)**, remember to give clear advice, i.e. stating 'agree' or 'disagree' (either answer is acceptable).

Exam tip

In order to make sure you are improving your performance in this topic, you should:

- focus on any mistakes you have made

- cross out any irrelevant points

- write in any points you overlooked (but make sure you understand these points fully)

- keep your answer for future reference; it could be helpful when you do your final revision.

5. The following ratios are available about a business:

	2017	2018
Gross margin	48%	43%
Profit margin	11%	9%

What has happened comparing 2018 with 2017? **(1)**

A	control of expenses has declined	**C**	purchases have been increased
B	control of expenses has improved	**D**	purchases have been reduced

6. Which ratio shows how well a business uses its resources? **(1)**

A	current ratio	**C**	rate of inventory turnover
B	liquid (acid test) ratio	**D**	return on capital employed

(Total marks: 6)

Structured questions

1. Ravi uses ratios to assess his business's profitability.

    (a) Explain how ratios can help Ravi assess profitability. **(2)**

    Ravi has provided the following details about his business for the year ended 31 December 2018:

	$ 000
Administrative expenses	13
Carriage inwards	4
Carriage outwards	6
Depreciation charges	29
Inventory	
1 January 2018	15
31 December 2018	13
Purchases	144
Rent received	8
Returns inwards	3
Revenue	282
Selling expenses	10

    Additional information at 31 December 2018 is as follows:

	$ 000
Current assets	38
Current liabilities	27
Non-current assets	440
Non-current liabilities	60

    (b) Calculate the following ratios to 2 decimal places: **(8)**

    i.   gross margin

    ii. profit margin

    iii. return on capital employed.

2. Anita wishes to assess her business's performance for the year ended 31 December 2018.

   (a) What is the difference between the current ratio and the liquid (acid test) ratio? **(2)**

   Anita has provided the following details.

   For the year ended 31 December 2018:

	$
Expenses	38 300
Inventory	
1 January 2018	13 500
31 December 2018	11 500
Purchases	132 300
Revenue	197 400

   At 31 December 2018:

	$
Bank loan (repayable 2024)	25 000
Capital (1 January 2018)	88 000
Cash at bank	6 600
Drawings	18 500
Inventory	11 500
Non-current assets at net book value	97 300
Trade payables	12 200
Trade receivables	16 100

   Additional information: all purchases and sales are on a credit basis.

   (b) Calculate the following ratios: **(11)**

   i. current ratio

   ii. liquid (acid test) ratio

   iii. rate of inventory turnover

   iv. trade receivable days

   v. trade payable days.

3. Yasmin owns a wholesale business. She uses ratios to analyse her financial statements.

   (a) State **three** external users who might also wish to analyse the financial statements of Yasmin's business. **(3)**

   Yasmin has presented the following information about two recent years:

	Year ended 30 June 2017	Year ended 30 June 2018
Gross margin	50%	55%
Profit margin	18%	22%
Return on capital employed	8%	11%
Rate of inventory turnover	11 times	9 times
Trade receivables turnover	33 days	39 days

(b) State which ratios show a decline in the business's performance since 30 June 2017. **(2)**

(c) Explain **one** reason why the gross margin has changed from 50% to 55% since 30 June 2017. **(2)**

(d) State **three** possible reasons for the increase in the profit margin since 30 June 2017. **(3)**

(e) Explain **two** reasons why the rate of inventory turnover has changed since 30 June 2017. **(4)**

(f) Describe **one** possible result of the change in the trade receivables turnover since 30 June 2017. **(2)**

(g) Yasmin would like to improve the business's rate of inventory turnover. Recommend two ways in which the rate of inventory turnover could be improved. **(2)**

4. Yeung, a furniture retailer, has been comparing his business's performance with two other businesses for the year ended 31 December 2018.

(a) State **three** factors Yeung should consider when deciding which businesses to choose in order to make valid comparisons. **(3)**

The following information is available:

	Yeung's business	Business A	Business B
Profit margin	12%	14%	15%
Return on capital employed	9%	7%	7%
Current ratio	1.9:1	2.3:1	2.2:1
Liquid (acid test) ratio	1.4:1	1.5:1	1.3:1
Trade payables turnover	33 days	32 days	29 days
Trade receivables turnover	27 days	31 days	32 days

Additional information: these are the normal ratios for furniture retailers:

Current ratio	2.2:1
Liquid (acid test) ratio	1.3:1
Trade payables turnover	30 days
Trade receivables turnover	30 days

(b) State which business has the best liquidity ratios. Give reasons for your choice. **(3)**

(c) Give **one** reason Yeung's business has the best return on capital employed although it has lowest profit margin. **(2)**

(d) Explain **one** way in which Business A could improve its current ratio. **(2)**

(e) State **three** ways in Yeung could improve his liquid (acid test) ratio. **(3)**

(f) State **one** way in which Business A could improve its trade receivables turnover. **(1)**

Yeung is pleased with his business's trade payables turnover and trade receivables turnover.

(g) Advise Yeung whether or not he should be pleased with these ratios. Give reasons for your advice. **(5)**

(Total marks: 60)

Unit 7:
Accounting principles, policies and standards

Unit outline

Accounting statements are used by a wide range of interested parties to help them make decisions about aspects of a business's performance. It is important that accounting information is accurate, and that users feel confident it would be the same whoever prepared it.

Accounting principles and policies are designed to give this assurance to interested parties.

Either tick these boxes to build a record of your revision, or use them to identify your strengths and weaknesses.

Your revision checklist

Specification	☺	😐	☹
7.1 Accounting principles, policies and standards			

You will need to know how to:

- explain the following accounting principles: business entity, consistency, duality, going concern, historic cost, matching, materiality, money measurement, prudence and realization
- explain the following accounting policies: comparability, relevance, reliability and understandability.

Many of the fundamental rules which are used to ensure accounting information is prepared in the same way by everyone have already been introduced at relevant points in this book. The following table summarizes the main points about each principle.

Explanation	Examples
Business entity	
Only matters that affect the financial position of a business are included in the business's records. Any private financial transactions of the owner should not be recorded. In other words, a sole trader business and the owner's private affairs are seen as two different entities. The links between the two separate entities are (in the case of a sole trader) the capital account and drawings accounts in the business's books of account.	• A business's records should not include any transactions relating to the owner of the business. For example: payments from the owner's *private* bank account for electricity costs relating to the owner's home. • If the owner paid for insurance for his or her home from the *business* bank account, this would need to be recorded as drawings in the business's books of account.
Consistency	
The accounting methods or policies used by a business should be used in the same way in each accounting period. This principle is designed to make sure that one year's results for a business can be fairly compared to that for any other year. If this were not the case, any comparisons would be distorted by figures resulting from changes in methods or policies.	• The same method of depreciation is used for a particular non-current asset each year. • The same rate of depreciation is used for a particular non-current asset each year. • The same rate of provision for doubtful debts is maintained each year.
Duality	
Every transaction is regarded as having two aspects and this is the basis for maintaining day-to-day accounting records.	• If an asset is purchased, the bank account (if payment is made immediately) or the account of a supplier is affected (if the purchase is made on credit). • If a sale of goods is made then a record is made in a sales account, but a second entry is also made in either the cash/bank account (if money is received immediately) or in the account of a trade receivable (if the goods are sold on credit).
Going concern	
This is based on the idea that a business's existence is assumed to continue indefinitely. As a result, assets are always valued at their cost rather than their potential market value, since it is assumed the assets will be continue to be used by the business for the foreseeable future.	• A delivery vehicle is valued at its cost (less depreciation to date) even if it could be potentially sold for a much higher value. • Some furniture and fittings are shown in the statement of financial position at cost less accumulated depreciation, even if they would have little or no second-hand value if sold.

Historic cost	
It is desirable that accounting information is as factual as possible (objective) rather than based on someone's opinion (subjective).	• Each non-current asset is valued at cost and depreciation charges are based on this cost figure.
As a result, all transactions are recorded at their cost of purchase as these values can be verified by checking with the source documents.	• The starting point for valuing inventories is to value each item at cost rather than the sale price or the replacement price.
It should be noted that one problem does arise: an item purchased some time ago could have quite a different cost from the same item purchased now. This is because of the effect of inflation.	

Matching	
Costs and revenues should be matched to the same accounting period. Costs and revenues are matched whether or not amounts have been actually paid or received. This principle is sometimes referred to as the 'accruals principle'.	Making adjustments in income statements for: • expense accruals • expense prepayments • income due • income received in advance, depreciation • provisions for doubtful debts • opening and closing inventories.

Materiality	
The concept seeks to avoid valuable time being wasted trying to apply the usual accounting concepts to items of small value or of minimal importance to a business. These items are often grouped together and written off immediately rather than being recorded as non-current assets and depreciated over their useful life.	• Small-value assets are recorded as expenses in the year of purchase rather non-current assets which are then subject to depreciation, for example office items such as staplers and calculators.
Each business must decide on a cut-off point at which low-value items should be regarded as immaterial (i.e. insignificant). For a large business this could be set at $1,000 or an even higher figure; for a small business the figure could be much lower.	• Minor expense items are grouped together in a general expenses account rather than appearing as separate expenses in the nominal ledger and income statement. • A mobile phone could be written off by a large business, but could be included as office equipment by a small business.

Money measurement	
Financial records only include items which have a monetary value.	Some key features of a successful business are not recorded in the accounts and financial statements, such as: • managerial expertise • staff efficiency • customer relations • location.

Prudence	
To avoid users believing a business is performing better than is really the case, it is important that profits and asset values are not overstated (or losses and liabilities understated). If so, losses are written off as soon as they become apparent, but profits are not recorded until they are certain. If an optimistic view is given about a business's profits, decisions could be taken which are not justified. For example, excessive drawings could be made by the owner. The prudence principle is regarded as one of the most important rules. It must be applied whenever there is doubt about a value, even if this means ignoring other accounting principles. The prudence principles is sometimes referred to as 'conservatism'.	• Irrecoverable debts are written off as soon as they become apparent. • Provisions for doubtful debts are created where there is thought to be a risk of irrecoverable debts. • Inventory is valued at the lower of cost and net realizable value.
Realization	
Revenue is only recorded in the accounting records when payment is received or when the promise of payment is made. This ensures profits are not overstated and they are recorded only when there is certainty that the value will be received.	• A sale is recorded when cash is received from the customer. • A credit sale is recorded when an invoice is issued. • An order from a customer is not recorded as a sale because the order could be cancelled by the customer, or the supplier may not be able to fulfill the order.

Much work has been done in recent years to establish some international accounting standards to ensure users of accounting information can be sure of the quality of financial statements presented by businesses. These international standards have been adopted in the majority of countries worldwide.

How accounting information can be judged for quality

Factor	Explanation
Comparability	Accounting information should be comparable within a business from one year to another. Accounting information should be comparable from one business to another similar business. To ensure comparisons can be made, any changes in methods should be made apparent and the effects of these changes should be made known.
Relevance	Users of accounting information need to be certain that what is presented has been designed to meet their needs.
Reliability	Accounting information can be depended upon if it is free from: • significant errors • bias (i.e. it is unfairly weighted in favour of, or against, a particular view).
Understandability	For accounting information to be understandable it must be: • clear • capable of being grasped by those with a satisfactory knowledge of accounting and who are willing to study the information provided with some diligence • prepared with the needs of users in mind. It is worth noting that those who prepare accounting statements must not withhold information on the basis that it might be too complex for the user to understand.

⏪ Recap

1. Accounting principles provide guidance on how to treat transactions and prepare financial statements.

2. They help to ensure users of accounting information can have confidence that the details would be the same whoever had prepared the records.

3. Those analysing financial statements can be reasonably sure that they can make valid and meaningful decisions based on the information the statements contain.

4. Accounting standards have been developed to ensure accounting information is comparable, relevant, reliable and easy to understand.

Exam tip

It is not easy to remember the terms used in accounting principles. It may help to think of a mnemonic device to help you.

✏️ Apply

1. Abdulrahman has been advised to create a provision for doubtful debts. State two accounting principles which he will apply.

2. When Bibek purchased a machine the purchase price was used to record the value of asset in the books of account. State which accounting principle was being applied.

3. Bibek has provided depreciation on the machine each financial year and has used the same method of depreciation each year. State two accounting principles which have been applied when charging depreciation.

4. Identify the four key ways in which accounting information can be judged for quality based on international standards.

⏱️ Review

There is more about accounting principles in sections 7.1–7.3 of *Essential Accounting for Cambridge IGCSE® & O Level (third edition)*, pages 315–21.

Exam-style questions

1. A trainee accountant has been preparing some draft financial statements for a business. The trainee has asked for advice about the following situations:

   (a) It appears that insurance has been paid covering the business into the first few months of the next financial year. **(3)**

   (b) An order for some goods has been recorded in the business's sales journal. **(3)**

   (c) The closing inventory has been valued at cost, but there are some items which are damaged, and can only be sold for a price below cost. **(3)**

   (d) The statement of financial position includes some items of furniture which, because of their age and quality, have been recorded at a high resale price. **(3)**

   (e) Some small items of office equipment of low value have been purchased this year, and are likely to be of use in the business for several years to come. **(3)**

   (f) The owner has suggested switching to the reducing-balance method of depreciation as this will be less than the depreciation charge using the straight-line method. **(3)**

   (g) The business's rent account includes payments that also cover the owner's private apartment above the main business premises. **(3)**

   Advise the trainee accountant how to treat each of the situations.

   Before you answer the question **(Total marks: 21)**

   Remember it is important to identify the most relevant accounting principle to be applied in each case.

   It is usually recommended that as well as identifying a principle, there should be a brief description of the what the principle means.

   Remember to be precise when giving answers. For example, it is not enough to state that something should be recorded in the assets section of a statement of financial position. Instead, state under which subheading the item should be recorded: current assets or non-current assets.

Check your answer

1. **(a)** Matching principle **(1)**: the amount of the insurance which is prepaid (i.e. relates to the next financial period) should not be recorded in the income statement **(1)** but should appear as an account receivable in the current assets section of the statement of financial position **(1)**.

(b) Realization principle **(1)**: the order should not have been recorded in the sales journal as no sale has yet been confirmed **(1)**; it will be necessary to cancel entries arising from posting the order to the sales account and the account of trade receivables **(1)**.

(c) Prudence principle **(1)**: the inventory should have been recorded at the lower of cost or net realizable value **(1)**, so the inventory valuation should be reduced which will also reduce the gross profit for the year (and profit for the year) **(1)**.

(d) Going concern principle **(1)**: the furniture should be recorded as cost less depreciation charges **(1)** and the resale value ignored as it can be assumed the furniture will continue to be used in the business **(1)**.

(e) Materiality principle **(1)**: the items should be written off as an expense in this year's income statement **(1)** as it would not be worthwhile to record the items as non-current assets and calculate annual depreciate charges **(1)**.

(f) Consistency principle **(1)**: the straight-line method should continue to be used **(1)** to ensure this year's income statement can be compared with previous years' income statements in a meaningful way **(1)**.

(g) Business entity principle **(1)**: the private transactions of the owner should not be recorded in the expense accounts of the business **(1)**; the rent on the private apartment should be debited to the drawings account **(1)**.

Multiple choice questions

1. Raju has made the following entries for some goods taken for own use: Dr Drawings, Cr Purchases.

Which accounting principle did Raju apply? (1)

A consistency   C going concern

B duality   D matching

> **Exam tip**
>
> If you made any errors, go back and write in some corrections and any points overlooked. It is a good idea to write a note about why the model answer was correct and why your answer was not.

> ⊗ **Common errors**
>
> Remember to:
>
> - identify the relevant principle
>
> - give the correct and full name for a principle: for example, don't write 'entity principle' rather than 'business entity principle'
>
> - give a full description of how to treat the situation. For example, in **(a)** you must cover both the income statement and the statement of financial position.

2. Chana has made entries to record recent receivables due but unpaid at the end of her business's financial year.

Which accounting principle did Chana apply? **(1)**

A business entity   **C** prudence

B matching   **D** realization

3. A business's inventory included an item which had cost $430 and which was due to be sold for $560. The item was slightly damaged, but after repairs costing $80 it was expected to be sold for $530.

How should the item be valued in the business's inventory? **(1)**

A $560   **B** $530   **C** $480   **D** $430

(Total marks: 3)

Structured questions

1. Henri recently prepared his business's end of year financial statements. The income statement included adjustments for:

- inventory valued at the lower of cost or net realizable value
- provision for doubtful debts
- insurance prepaid.

(a) Explain **two** accounting concepts which Henri applied when making these adjustments. **(4)**

(b) Identify **two** other accounting concepts which should be applied when preparing an income statement. **(2)**

(c) Explain why it is important for financial statements to be comparable. **(3)**

2. Morad is responsible for preparing a business's accounting records. He is unsure how to record the following:

i. A trade receivable's account has been outstanding for many months and it seems unlikely payment will now be received.

ii. His skilful workforce has been behind much of the business's success, so Morad believes this to be one of his business's most valuable assets.

iii. The business's motor vehicle expenses account has been debited with all the payments made for fuel and servicing during the year. Half of the vehicle's mileage is accounted for by trips for private purposes.

iv. The rent received account includes an amount received from the tenant which covers the first two months of the next financial year.

(a) Explain why accounting principles are important. **(2)**

(b) Explain to Morad how each of these items should be treated. **(12)**

(Total marks: 23)

Account payable	A current liability arising from an accrued expense
Account receivable	A current asset arising from a prepaid expense
Accounting equation	The formula which links assets, liabilities and owner's equity (capital)
Accounting	The selecting, classifying and summarizing of financial data in ways that provide the owners of businesses (and others) with useful information to help them assess performance and plan future activities
Accrued expense	An amount unpaid for an expense during an accounting period
Accumulated fund	The total of a club's surpluses over a period of years (equivalent of a business's capital)
Aging schedule of trade receivables	A list of all amounts due from credit customers shown in a sequence based on how long the debt has been outstanding
Appropriation account	A financial statement which details how profits or losses have been shared between partners
Asset	A resource with a monetary value which is owned by a business
Bank statement	A copy of a customer's bank account, sent to the customer by the bank at regular intervals
Bookkeeping	The recording of financial information, particularly transactions, in a systematic way
Business entity	A type of business, such as a corporation or limitied liability company. To refer to the business entity is to separate the activity of the business from the individuals (e.g. employees, owners or managers) associated with it
Capital	The investment made by the owner of the business
Capital employed	The total funds used by a business made up of capital plus non-current liabilities (or alternatively total assets less current liabilities)
Capital expenditure	Money spent on non-current assets which is intended to be of benefit for more than one financial year
Capital receipt	Money received from one-off non-trading activities
Consistency	Policies adopted for recording financial information should continue to be used year-on-year
Contra entry	When a business deals with another business or organization both as a customer and as a supplier, the balance of the two accounts are set off against one another to find the net balance
Credit transfer	The automatic transfer of funds into a business's bank account by one of the business's credit customers
Current account	Records the day-to-day changes in a partner's investment in a business arising from drawings and profits/losses
Current asset	An asset which is quickly turned into cash and is of benefit to the business for short term (less than one year)
Current liability	A liability which will be settled in the near future (less than one year)

Deed of partnership	A formal agreement between partners covering how profits and losses will be shared and the rules under which partners will work together
Depreciation	The loss in value of a non-current asset over its useful life
Direct cost	Manufacturing costs which are attributable to a single product
Direct debit	Where authority is given to a bank by a customer to make payments on its behalf to another organization
Dishonoured cheque	A cheque which a bank will not accept for payment because the individual making the payment does not have enough funds in his or her account to cover the amount being paid
Duality	Every transaction has two aspects, requiring two entries in an accounting system
Equity	The value of a company's share capital and reserves
Factory overheads	The total of all factory indirect costs
Fixed capital account	Records the agreed and unchanging capital contribution of a partner
Going concern	A business which will continue to be in existence for the foreseeable future
Goods for own use	Owner's drawings in the form of inventory
Goodwill	The additional value of an established and successful business, above the value of its tangible assets
Historic cost	Transactions recorded using the actual cost of purchase
Income and expenditure account	An annual summary which shows whether a club made a surplus or deficit
Indirect cost	A manufacturing cost which cannot be attributed to one product
Intangible asset	An asset which has a monetary value but which does not have physical presence
Interest on capital	A reward where a partner is awarded interest based on the individual's capital contribution
Interest on drawings	A penalty where a partner is charged interest based on the amount of drawings taken during a financial year
Irrecoverable debt	An amount owed by a credit customer which will not be paid
Liability	An amount owed by a business to another individual, business or organization
Limited liability	The liability of any shareholder for the debts of the company is limited to the amount of the individual's fully paid shares
Manufacturing account	The first part of the annual financial statements of a manufacturing organization, which shows the total cost of producing goods
Matching	Profits are based on matching the revenues for a period with the expenses for that period irrespective of whether money has been received or paid

Matching principle	The revenue for an accounting period is matched with the costs for that accounting period
Materiality	The importance or significance of an amount, transaction or discrepancy
Money measurement	Only transactions which have a monetary value are recorded
Net book value	The cost of a non-current asset less the total depreciation to date
Net realizable value	The estimated sale value less any costs incurred in ensuring the goods are in a saleable condition
Non-current asset	An asset which should be of benefit to the business for a long time (more than one year)
Non-current liability	A liability which will be settled in the longer term (more than one year)
Owner's equity	The investment made by the owner(s) of a business; often referred to as 'capital'
Partnership salary	A reward in the form of a share of profits for undertaking some particular responsibility in the management of the business
Partnership	A form of business ownership where two or more individuals work together with the view to making a profit
Prepaid expense	An amount paid for an expense which covers part of the next accounting period
Prime cost	The total of all direct costs
Provision for doubtful debts	An amount set aside from profits to take account of the likelihood that some trade receivables will not pay the amount due
Prudence	Where there is doubt that asset and profit values are understated and losses and liabilities are overstated
Purchases ledger control account	A technique for checking the arithmetical accuracy of the purchases ledger
Realization	A sale is recorded when the customer pays or when an invoice is issued
Receipts and payments account	An annual summary of a cash book
Recovery of debt	When a debt which has previously been written off is paid
Reducing-balance method	A fixed percentage of the net book value of the asset is charged as depreciation each year
Residual value	The value of a non-current asset at the end of its useful life
Revaluation method	The annual depreciation charge is based on comparing the value of the asset at the year end with the value at the beginning of the year
Revenue expenditure	Money spent on running costs which benefits only the current financial year
Revenue receipt	Money received from normal business activity
Sales ledger control account	A technique for checking the arithmetical accuracy of the sales ledger

Glossary

Standing order	Where a customer gives a bank instructions to make an automatic payment to another organization of a fixed amount at regular intervals
Statement of affairs	Summary of a business's assets, liabilities and capital at a given date (the format resembles a summarized statement of financial position)
Straight-line method	The cost of an asset less estimated residual value, spread evenly over the estimated useful life of the asset
Suspense account	A temporary account used to make the totals of a trial balance agree
Trade payable	An amount owed by a business to supplier who has provided goods or services on credit
Trade receivable	An amount owed to a business by a customer who has been provided with goods or services on credit
True and fair	The principle that accounting records should be factually accurate and present a reasonable estimate of the financial position
Uncredited deposit	An amount paid into a bank account but which has not yet been recorded on the bank statement as a credit entry
Unpresented cheque	A cheque which has not been cleared by the bank and has not, therefore, been recorded on a customer's bank statement
Work in progress	Partly finished goods

	Revision Period 1	Revision Period 2	Revision Period 3	Revision Period 4	Revision Period 5	Revision Period 6
Sunday						
Saturday						
Friday						
Thursday						
Wednesday						
Tuesday						
Monday						

	Revision Period 1	Revision Period 2	Revision Period 3	Revision Period 4	Revision Period 5	Revision Period 6
Sunday						
Saturday						
Friday						
Thursday						
Wednesday						
Tuesday						
Monday						